FLYING MODERN JET FIGHTERS

Read what it takes to be a successful combat pilot, and share first-hand the exhilaration of flying a wide variety of aircraft — from Phantom to F-111.

FLYING MODERN JET FIGHTERS

ROBERT JACKSON

Patrick Stephens, Wellingborough

Distributed by
STERLING PUBLISHING CO., INC.
Two Park Avenue
New York, N. Y. 10016

Page 6 *Leading edge root extensions, plus a quarter of a ton of lead in the tail, turn BAe's 'fly-by-wire' active control demonstrator Jaguar into an agile performer. The aircraft is seen here returning to Warton after showing its paces at Farnborough in September 1984.*

First published in 1986

British Library Cataloguing in Publication Data

Jackson, Robert, 1941-
   Flying modern jet fighters.
   1. Fighter planes—Piloting
   I. Title
   623.74'64   TL685.3

   ISBN 0-85059-713-7

Patrick Stephens Limited is part of the Thorsons Publishing Group

Printed and bound in Great Britain.

Contents

Acknowledgements

I have received help from a lot of people in preparing this book, but I must express particular thanks to John S. Godden, Deputy PR Manager of British Aerospace Weybridge Division for photographic and other material on the Harrier and Hawk, and also to Mandy Penistone of BAe Warton for similar material on the Jaguar and Tornado. I am grateful to Dr Bob McManners for the explanatory drawings of air combat manoeuvres. I am also indebted to Bill Gunston for his help with the chapter on the F-111. The quote by Colonel Bob White, USAF, on flying the X-15 comes from a transcript of a lecture given by him to the Test Pilots' Group of the Royal Aeronautical Society in 1964, with due acknowledgement to that source.

Chapter 1
Schools for combat

It is dawn, and all except for one small corner the sun rises over an America at peace.

The corner is Nellis Air Force Base, Nevada, where the pilots of six Jaguars are preparing to go to war. The Jaguars are visitors from Royal Air Force Strike Command; their normal base is Coltishall, set amid the lush farmlands of Norfolk, a world apart in every sense from the barren lunar landscape that stretches to the north of their present location.

Paradoxically, Nellis lies only eight miles to the north-east of the glittering lights of Las Vegas. Together with its associated bombing and gunnery ranges it extends across more than three million acres, which makes it the biggest USAF base — bigger even than the home countries of some of the foreign pilots who come here for combat training.

Named after Lieutenant William Nellis, a fighter pilot who was killed in action over Europe in 1944, the base is part of the USAF's Tactical Air Command and is run by over 10,000 personnel, mostly military. Its principal unit is the Tactical Fighter Weapons Centre, which is responsible for conducting advanced tactical fighter training and combat training under simulated war conditions for the USAF, US Navy, NATO and other allied air forces.

Intensive training of this nature is carried out over six-week periods several times a year under the name of Exercise Red Flag. The procedure was begun in the 1970s by General Robert Dixon, at that time commander of TAC, and was born out of the Vietnam War, which had shown that no matter how thorough a pilot's training might be, it by no means covered all the situations he was likely to encounter in combat. Experience remedied that deficiency, and after ten operational missions a pilot was well equipped to survive in a hostile environment.

Some pilots, however, never reached the ten-mission mark. That was why Red Flag was instituted: to raise a pilot's experience to somewhere in the region of the ten-mission level and therefore immeasurably increase his chances of combat survival.

The pilot's controlled and realistic initiation to combat at Nellis takes place within a vast area. The Red Flag 'playpen' encompasses a ten-million-acre block of airspace reserved exclusively for military flying. Within it lie the three million acres that constitute the actual range area. The range includes fifty different types of target, including airfields and industrial complex outlines, two vehicle convoys — one of which is more than seventeen miles long, correctly spaced and protected by tracked anti-aircraft guns — ten miles of railway with a ten-car train, and armoured replicas of Soviet T-62 tanks deployed for battle.

These targets are defended by thirty-five threat simulators which are visually, and in most cases electronically, similar to Soviet-built equipment. Organised into two Brigades, early warning radars detect aircraft at 300 miles and pass data to the Red Force Filter Centre at the Range Control Centre. The latter is situated at Indian Springs Air Force Auxiliary Field, forty-five miles north-west of Las Vegas; this is the home of the 554th Support Squadron of the 554th Range Group, and the 350 personnel based there provide bombing and gunnery range support for the tactical air operations out of Nellis. They also, incidentally, provide support backup for the US Department of Energy's nuclear weapons testing programme.

The Filter Centre relays its information to Red Force Brigade commanders who initiate defensive operations. More than fourteen different types of radar units simulate those used by Warsaw Pact countries, operating at the same frequencies, pulse widths, pulse repetition roles, scan patterns and power levels. TV cameras are fitted to many of these units to cover the same area as the radar; other instruments report factors such as threat switch positions and transmit to Range Control.

All data collected on the range is processed by computers which can generate not only plots of an engagement or of a single aircraft's entire mission, but also several kinds of two- or three- dimensional graphic displays from different perspectives. When pilots return from a sortie, the Range Control Centre provides computer plots of the mission; pilots can view video tapes of their aircraft as seen in the sights of enemy surface-to-air missile controllers, anti-aircraft guns or camera-gun film shot by aggressor aircraft.

The latter are predominantly Northrop F-5Es and T-38s of the 57th Tactical Training Wing, whose two squadrons — the 64th and 65th — fly aircraft camouflaged in patterns typical of Warsaw Pact machines. They are flown by some of the best fighter pilots in the US Air Force, men skilled in Warsaw Pact tactics, and they constitute a formidable 'enemy'. They share Nellis with the 474th Tactical Fighter Wing, which flies F-16 Fighting Falcons — as does Nellis' most famous resident unit, the Thunderbirds USAF aerobatic team.

It has taken the Jaguars four days to reach Nellis, staging through Lossiemouth, then across the great circle route to Goose Bay, then on over the North American continent to reach their destination via Loring AFB, Maine, Rickenbacker AFB, and McConnell AFB in Kansas. The westabout detachment has required considerable support from Victor K.2s of the RAF Tanker Wing, Marham, and from teams of technical personnel, deployed to the various stopover points by Hercules transports, but RAF detachments to Nellis are now a matter of routine and the procedure is firmly established. At Nellis, the supporting ground crews participate in a less-publicised part of the overall exercise; code-named Black Flag, it tests their ability and efficiency in keeping their aircraft flying under what amounts to hectic wartime conditions.

In the Jaguar, the RAF has a fine aircraft for the task in hand. Because of its relatively small camouflaged profile, the aircraft is extremely hard to detect with the naked eye, even against a desert background. In addition, the Jaguar's low gust response and excellent handling-characteristics enable it to fly extremely low at transonic speed, presenting further problems for defending fighters; it also produces a very small signature on radar monitors and this, coupled with its speed and height, produces intermittent radar returns which tend to merge with ground clutter or be missed completely.

The Jaguar GR1 is a single-seat strike aircraft whose principal role is the direct tactical support of ground forces. It has three main weapon stations, one under the fuselage centreline and one under each wing. Each of these weapon points can carry up to 1,134 kg of offensive stores or external fuel. In addition, the Jaguar GR 1 has two 30 mm Aden guns mounted under the aircraft, just aft of the cockpit.

The Jaguar's cockpit is neat and compact and reflects the close co-operation that existed between its manufacturers and the air forces whose pilots were destined to use it. It is, however, noisy, compelling the pilot to shout into the microphone of his Plessey PTR377 V/UHF radio to make himself heard above the background noise. Transmissions, especially between Jaguars in close formation, can sometimes be difficult to make out.

In all other respects, the Jaguar's avionics are excellent. The Jaguar GR 1's whole raison d'etre is to deliver its weapon load on to its target with pinpoint accuracy, and for this task it is fitted with two weapon guidance systems: a Laser Ranging and Marked Target Seeker (LRMTS) and a Navigation and Weapon Aiming Subsystem (NAVWASS), both developed by Ferranti.

The core of NAVWASS is the FIN 1064 inertial navigator, whose control and display unit is mounted on the cockpit coaming. Using a keyboard, the pilot punches in data that includes the latitudes and longitudes of datum, waypoint, initial point and target, groundspeed, bank angle at weapon release, initial fuel load, fuel burn, runway direction, minimum fuel on return and attack data. All this is done as part of the pre-flight checks. The system continuously computes the impact point, the relevant information being fed to the pilot via a head-up display.

The Continuously-Computed Impact Point mode takes velocity, slant range, altitude and ballistic inputs and calculates the impact point for guns, bombs or rockets. The impact point is displayed on the HUD, and when the sight mark crosses the target the pilot

A Jaguar GR 1 of No 54 Squadron, RAF Coltishall, flown by Wing Commander R.J. Kemball, the squadron commander, and carrying two 1,200 litre fuel tanks and four 1,000 lb bombs.

Jaguar GR 1 of No 6 Squadron, RAF Coltishall, carrying six 1,000 lb bombs, four under the wings and two under the fuselage centreline. The aircraft is flown by No 6's CO, Wing Commander Neil Hayward.

manually releases his weapons. The other available mode is the Continuously-Computed Release Point. In this, the sight mark on the head-up display is depressed a few degrees. When the mark hits the target, the pilot initiates weapons release. The ranging sensor, slaved to the sight reticle, takes an instantaneous slant range measurement. The pilot starts to pull up and the computer begins calculating target range based on the initial velocity, range and ballistic inputs. Range to bomb impact point is also computed. When the two ranges coincide the weapons are released automatically.

Of the two modes, CCIP allows more flexibility of targeting and is often preferred for close support when targets are numerous. CCRP comes into its own with inertial systems where the pilot is guided to a pre-selected target, based on co-ordinates entered before take-off or during the flight. If the system is sufficiently accurate the pilot can drop his bombs without seeing the target.

Both modes require accurate range information, and this is where the laser rangefinder comes in. LRMTS, whose principal sensor is mounted in the Jaguar's chisel-shaped nose section, is designed to be used in conjunction with a ground-based laser target designator.

In the British Army, this is the Laser Target Marker and Ranger (LTMR) which is tripod-mounted and also developed by Ferranti. The aircraft-mounted LRMTS consists of a gimballed seeker which scans a cone forward of the aircraft, searching for reflected laser radiation from the LTMR; once a designated target is picked up, the seeker locks on and target position is displayed on the pilot's HUD. Slant range to the target is measured by firing a laser beam at the target and measuring the time taken for the reflected radiation to return. In rain, illuminated targets can be detected at a range of 2 km; this rises to 6 km in mist, and under ideal conditions — a clear, frosty morning, for example — the acquisition range can rise to 18 km.

To indicate enemy radar activity in a hostile environment, the Jaguar is fitted with a radar warning receiver, a piece of equipment more sophisticated than it sounds. There are an enormous number of radar systems in use, and if the receiver warned the pilot of every signal it picked up it would create endless false alarms. The Jaguar's RWR, the Marconi Space and Defence Systems ARI 18223, consequently incorporates a degree of signal processing so that only those signals representing a threat to the aircraft are displayed, the information being presented to the pilot by lamps on a display unit. Forward- and rearward-facing antennae for the system are mounted on the vertical fin of the aircraft. To break radar lock, the Jaguar's pilot relies primarily on the masking effect of the terrain over which he is flying at very low level, but the aircraft can also carry a chaff dispenser — developed by RAF ground crews at Bruggen, in West Germany — in place of the normal braking parachute.

Power for the Jaguar GR 1 is provided by a pair of Rolls-Royce/Turbomeca Adour Mk 104 turbojets, which develop 27 per cent more thrust than the original Mk 102 engines. Jaguar was designed, without compromise, for an ultra-low-level role for which prime requirements were high wing loading to cut through turbulence and a bypass engine to achieve good fuel economy for long ranges; this produced an aircraft outstanding for the ground-attack role but, inevitably, lacking the exceptional thrust and turning performance of specialized combat fighters. The adoption of the Mk 104 engine has gone a long way towards improving that position and realising the Jaguar's full potential in RAF service.

Jaguar has increased considerably in complexity and weight since it was first conceived, and the aircraft's handling has been greatly improved, mainly through the addition of electronic systems. There was a problem, in the early days, with very heavy stick forces experienced at high airspeeds while pulling g with underwing stores. These forces (up to 20 lb/g) contrasted very unfavourably with the comparatively light 2 lb/g recorded at low speed and without stores. After many possible solutions were tried, the problem was solved by lowering the top speed at which the aircraft's 'Ajax' artificial-feel system stopped feeding back force increases to the control column. Low-speed forces remained unaltered, but an increase in the 'Ajax' low-speed cut-off could raise them if necessary.

The wartime role of the RAF's Jaguar squadrons in NATO's front line in Germany is to help stem any armoured/infantry thrusts against Forward Defended Localities (FDLs). To carry out this function they have to survive a surprise air strike on their bases, and so the Jaguars of each squadron are housed in nine hardened aircraft shelters, with three more shelters housing their supporting equipment, and two their fuel bowsers. The shelters, which can withstand a direct hit by anything up to a 1,000 lb bomb, face in different directions to make an attacker's approach as difficult as possible and to minimise the likelihood of bombs scoring direct hits on the doors, which are themselves shielded by roof extensions.

Two Jaguar GR 1 aircraft of No 20 Squadron, RAF Bruggen, Germany. XZ384, nearest the camera, is carrying eight 1,000 lb bombs, while XX959 is carrying Paveway laser-guided bombs on the inboard pylons, a Westinghouse AN/ALQ 101-10 ECM pod on the port outer and a Phimat chaff dispenser on the starboard outer pylon.

Squadron personnel are housed in a separate block incorporating hardened sections (Pilot Briefing Facilities) which are filtered for nuclear, chemical or biological fallout.

NATO's emphasis on the ability to survive a conventional attack means that aircraft, stores, fuel and men are all protected. Air-conditioning and all services in a HAS operate 24 hours a day, all the year round; the philosophy of operating from the HAS has developed so that people and Jaguars are brought out into the open only when absolutely necessary, for example during exercises and to some extent during normal peacetime training.

It is normal to have two Jaguars in one shelter, but they have to be slightly staggered and not a great deal of room is left. The technique for getting both out quickly has been brought to a fine art. Intake covers are left on the rearmost of the two while the outboard engine of the front aircraft is started for taxi-ing. Once he is outside the HAS, the lead pilot lights up the other engine while his number two lights up both and follows him out. In this way, no tractors have to be used until the aircraft return and have to be reversed into the HAS.

Drills have also been perfected to ensure that not a second is

A Jaguar GR 1 from British Aerospace Warton Division's airfield operating from a stretch of the M55 motorway near Blackpool. Aircraft such as Jaguar could operate from inprovised strips such as this in time of war, though landing might pose problems.

wasted in retuelling and rearming the Jaguars as they return between sorties to their base or, possibly, to forward dispersal areas such as stretches of a motorway or other improvised runways. Constant practice is required to maintain the very high standards set. This may take place at very short notice, under simulated CBW attack, in heavy rain, or even when under fire, with personnel being removed as token casualties. As an example of what a skilled RAF ground crew can do, here is what happened when a Jaguar of No 6 Squadron at Coltishall was armed with six 1,000 lb HE Mk 177 retarded bombs and 300 rounds of 30 mm ammunition, and refuelled for its next mission during an Operational Turnround (OTR) against the clock:

12:00.00   Aircraft arrives in revetments.
12:00.20   Aircraft turns in revetments.
12:00.52   Aircraft shuts down, bowser arrives, 1st and 2nd bombs approach.
12:01.50   Turnround commences. 1st bomb on, 2nd bomb about to be fitted. Bomb trolley in position, 300 rounds of ammunition being loaded.
12:02.45   2nd bomb on, 3rd bomb approaching.
12:03.55   3rd bomb on, 4th bomb approaching, ammunition loaded.
12:05.35   4th bomb on, 5th bomb being loaded, 6th bomb approaching, empty bomb trolley departing.
12:07.15   6th bomb being loaded, no-volts checks being carried out.
12:08.05   6th bomb on, no-volts checks complete, refuelling finished.
12:08.20   Turnround complete, bowser departs, bomb pins about to be removed, preparing for engine start.
12:10.20   Aircraft taxis out of revetments.

This is the kind of pace that ground crews have to maintain during Red Flag, too, turning their aircraft round in less time than it takes to drink a cup of hot coffee and smoke a cigarette. But the ground crews are expert, highly-trained men — the beneficiaries of what is perhaps the finest training system in the world; they know what to expect, and what is expected of them. So do their pilots. But for a Jaguar pilot carrying out a low-level strike, there is a whole set of problems to be faced, and the problems may change like lightning from one moment to the next.

Any combat pilot is faced with one stark and basic fact: that the enemy is a man who will try to kill you before you see him. The pilot of a heavily-laden strike aircraft such as the Jaguar has an additional problem in that his limited manoeuvring ability means that a potential threat must be sighted at long range if he and his aircraft are to survive. Although modern air-to-air missile ordnance has greatly increased the scope of an interceptor's attack geometry, the best attack position is still from the target's rear hemisphere, and if a fighter approaching from this direction is detected sufficiently early the pilot of the strike aircraft, even if the latter is fully laden, can still manoeuvre evasively enough to spoil the interceptor's attack geometry and place the enemy pilot in such a position that he is outside the performance parameters of the ordnance he carries.

Similarly, surface-to-air missiles can be avoided, particularly by low-flying aircraft, if they are visually detected soon after launch. The pilot must watch the missile's flight long enough to determine the SAM's characteristics and plan his evasive manoeuvres accordingly in order to frustrate the missile in its terminal guidance phase.

So let's return to Red Flag and see how it works in practice. The six Jaguar pilots involved have undergone a thorough briefing; the planning for each day's combat is necessarily complex, since a host of different aircraft types are all using the same block of airspace. Details such as which aircraft are to fly, their missions and broad timings are prepared weeks in advance, but the actual route, flight planning and tactics are left entirely to the individual mission commanders. It rests with them and the skill of their pilots as to whether or not the attack is successful.

Once airborne and en route, the Jaguars adopt a visual separation technique that not only enables the pilots to cover each other, but with good management will take all six aircraft through the target area in less than twenty seconds, saturating the objective with their practice bombs. Jaguar has been described as a 'forgiving' aircraft, and most competent pilots could fly it successfully from point A to point B, but to fly it in an Olympic-class exercise is another story, requiring immense concentration, stamina and skills found only in graduate-class pilots. The terrain-hugging technique, for example, sometimes requires a pilot to 'throw' his aircraft over a ridge on its back, rather like a high jumper, so that it never appears for more than a few seconds on the scope of a surveillance radar.

High over northern Scotland, a pair of Jaguar GR 1s from the OCU at Lossiemouth. This photograph shows a typical combat spacing.

The pilot must always be on the alert for a warning bleep and red light from his RWR which tells him that he is being tracked and that he must engage in violent manoeuvring, often involving negative 'g', to break lock. He needs to keep his eyes peeled for aggressor aircraft and, at the same time, keep Jaguar on track to its target through the information on his head-up display.

Somewhere out there are the aggressors, waiting to pounce, and learning how to spot them before they spot you is something that comes only with constant practice.

A combat pilot does not 'scan the sky' in the literal sense, at least not if he wants to stay alive. Instead, he divides the area to be examined into sectors, each of about 30°, and fixes his gaze on one sector before moving on to the next. Fixing the eye's gaze on a sector of sky is the whole of the secret, because only in this way can a pilot become aware of the relative motion of a tiny speck that may be either an aircraft or a missile, sighted at long range.

For the combat pilot, lack of focus is a constant problem. Unless he mentally instructs them to the contrary, his eyes will focus on a point anywhere between 6ft and 20ft outside the cockpit; the problem is at its most acute when the sky is eight-eighths blue, particularly deep blue. The trick is to focus on something in your sector of sky at the kind of range you would expect to pick up a threat, say between 3 and 7 nm. If there are clouds, fine; if not, the eye should be focused on an area of ground at the required distance, then moved up to search the appropriate sky sector. A common mistake is to search at too high an angle when the range is great; an angle of 45° and a range of seven miles combine to give an altitude of 30,000 ft, and there is small likelihood of a low-flying aircraft being detected visually from that flight level.

Once the speck that may or may not be a threat is sighted, the pilot must not take his eyes off it for an instant. Once the bogey — as unidentified and possibly hostile aircraft have been termed since the days of the Battle of Britain — has been checked out as such, and not a speck on the cockpit canopy or something else, the pilot's next action is to relate it to some nearby feature such as a cloud or landmark. Then, if it does go out of sight momentarily — say behind part of the cockpit structure — he should have no difficulty in re-locating it.

Operating at low level makes it easier to spot a bogey, especially when he is close to the horizon. Sometimes, the bogey will be leaving a distinctive smoke trail; the trail from a Phantom, for example, can be seen up to thirty miles away under certain lighting conditions, such as the afterglow of the sunset. If the smoke trail is suddenly cut off it means that the aircraft producing it has suddenly gone into reheat, which might mean that he has sighted you and is racing into the attack. Under other conditions, a glint in the sky from reflected sunlight may be the first indication that there is something out there.

Many modern combat aircraft, and the Jaguar is no exception, have poor rearward visibility that produces a blind cone in the six o'clock position. To check the dangerous rear area, the pilot has to weave constantly; small turns are enough, and may be accomplished even when flying down a narrow valley. Another alternative is to plan a route that includes frequent hard turns and eliminates long, straight legs. Whichever method is adopted, the pilot must keep his head on a constant swivel, and here a couple of factors are important. The first is the height of the seat, which should be adjusted to allow maximum visibility over the canopy sill and directly overhead; a pilot should always be able to tilt his head back to look above, and so the highest seat position that permits this is usually the best. Also, the pilot's helmet must fit properly; no part of it should impair vision, either at twelve o'clock high or on either side. In any case, an ill-fitting helmet is dangerous; not only can it slip embarrassingly if you have to swivel your head fast, but it can also break your neck if you have to bang out.

Another give-away of a bogey's presence is his shadow, assuming it's a sunny day and the terrain you are flying over is light in colour. The bogey must obviously be somewhere between his shadow and the sun, so to check the danger area the pilot places his thumb over the sun and then searches the sky around it. It goes without saying that no pilot ever looks into the sun without shielding it; anyone who does so is handing himself to the enemy on a plate.

During the Second World War, the great majority of pilots who were lost in air combat probably never saw the aircraft that shot them down. 'Sailor' Malan pointed that out forcefully in his famous ten commandments for air fighting, and it remains just as true

Jaguar has enjoyed considerable success in its 'International' export form. These photographs show the first two-seat International 'B' version for the Nigerian Air Force at Warton Aerodrome.

today. It is also true when dealing with surface-to-air missiles, something with which Second World War pilots did not have to contend. In the first few seconds after launch, a SAM's booster rocket leaves a thick grey or white smoke trail which can be easy to see even though the missile itself may be invisible; the smoke is usually accompanied by a vivid flame. Early SAMs like the SA-2 Guideline looked a bit like telephone poles perched on top of their columns of flame and smoke as they rose from the launch pad, but the defensive weaponry has since become smaller and more sophisticated. Even so, when the booster cuts out and the solid fuel sustainer engine takes over, the latter still produces a smoke trail that ranges from a dense white to a very thin grey. The transition from booster burn-out to sustainer, incidentally, means that guidance has begun. Liquid-fuelled missiles, on the other hand, emit very little smoke and flame and can be difficult to spot; fortunately, they are few and far between.

When the smoke trail takes on a wiggly appearance, it means the missile has entered its guidance phase. If the smoke and the bright light of the rocket exhaust remain at about the same spot on your canopy, the odds are that you are the target. This is because a guided SAM attempts to fly a lead pursuit course, holding its target at a constant angle. As SAMs are generally small, it is often difficult to estimate their range, so the sooner you take hard evasive action the better your chances of survival will be. Hard evasive action usually takes the form of high-g turns at very low level to break radar lock. Most airborne RWRs cover the E to J band; Soviet SAMs such as the SA-4 Ganef have long-range surveillance provided by an E-band Long Track radar whose beam is 7.5° in elevation and 3.5° in azimuth and which completes a scan every four seconds, while target acquisition and fire control are the responsibility of the H-band Pat Hand radar. A pilot, therefore, is warned to carry out evasive manoeuvres as soon as the RWR tells him that he is being tracked. No missiles are fired on a Red Flag exercise, of course, but the evasive tactics are the same as they would be in the real thing.

Heat-seeking SAMs such as the SA-7 and SA-9 have a much higher kill factor than their radio command-guided counterparts and present quite a different problem. They fly a pursuit course, and the likelihood is that they will be sighted at very short range, making immediate evasive action imperative. Because of the relatively low closure rate of a heat-seeker approaching from six o'clock, however, a pilot can spot its smoke trail quite near to his aircraft and still be able to break successfully. The odds are not so good when the missile is fired from a head-on position; if a pilot sees a missile trail curving towards him from his front quarter, he needs a lot of luck as well as skill to escape. Again, the best defence against heat-seeking missiles, the ground-launched variety at any rate, is evasive manoeuvring at very low level; SA-7, for example, is ineffective below 150 ft.

Heat-seeking missiles can also be thrown off track by infra-red flares, which are ejected from chaff dispensers. Early heat-seeking weapons were very vulnerable to this technique, but more recent designs use filters or dual operating frequencies to discriminate between the emissions from the hot metal of aircraft engines and those produced by flares.

For a Jaguar pilot attacking an enemy concentration at low level, the biggest threat to survival would in all probability come from anti-aircraft artillery (AAA) of which there is nowadays a formidable variety. As most AAA sites are heavily camouflaged, the first indication a pilot usually has of their presence is when he sees the muzzle flashes; large guns make big, slow-rate flashes, while small-bore rapid fire flashes produce a sparkling effect. Radar-directed guns do not generally use tracer ammunition, but small- and medium-calibre weapons that are visually laid use up to 25 per cent tracer rounds. In the heat of the action, a pilot may tend to forget, to his cost, that the tracer he sees represents only a

Jaguar International fitted with uprated Adour Dash 58 engines and armed with Matra Magic R550 AAMs demonstrates its ability to land on a grass strip. Jaguar is cleared to operate under similar conditions with a full military payload in excess of 10,000 lb.

fraction of the total ammunition that is being thrown in his direction. At dawn, dusk or night, if he is flying directly towards the gun, he may get the visual sensation that he is flying down a tunnel whose walls are made up of tracers; this can produce a mesmerising effect that makes the pilot reluctant to break for fear of hitting the 'wall' and consequently presents the gunners with some excellent no-deflection shooting. There have been occasions when pilots, apparently hypnotized, have flown down the stream and into the ground. If a pilot finds himself on the receiving end of airbursts, then he is the target of medium or heavy calibre AAA; small automatic weapons do not produce airbursts. If medium-calibre bursts occur between the aircraft and the gun, then the pilot has little to fear from that particular weapon; the bursts mark the limit of the gun's range. Heavy-calibre shells, on the other hand, generally employ proximity or radar fuses; the latter are probably in use if the altitude of the bursts changes as the target aircraft changes height during evasive manoeuvring.

Exercises like Red Flag can't give a pilot the feeling of what it is like to be sprayed by AAA, or to see a SAM curving towards him. What they can do is hone his weapons delivery accuracy to a fine degree under the stress of combat, and refine his evasive tactics. There's an apt saying at Nellis — the more you sweat in peace, the less you bleed in war — and the flying there is probably the most challenging a pilot will encounter in his entire career, short of actual combat. But Nellis is only one of the combat schools where pilots of the Western Alliance are put through their paces to ensure that they stay at least one step ahead of the potential opposition.

Exercise Maple Flag, which is centred on the Cold Lake Air Weapons Range at Alberta, Canada amid frozen lakes and silver birch forests, may best be described as a refrigerated version of Red Flag; in fact, it is run by Red Flag personnel from Nellis and is laid out along the same lines as the desert range, with missile and AAA sites to be avoided and dummy tanks and an airfield to be attacked. The difference is that Cold Lake, situated around 54° 30' North and 1,770 ft above sea level, offers the same weather conditions as those prevailing in north-west Europe, which are a long way from the sun-baked climes of the Nevada Desert. Even so, conditions at Cold Lake are generally clearer than those in Europe; the airfield can usually be seen from the air at a range of fifty miles.

The Maple Flag range, which measures 100 miles by forty, is virtually flat, which presents a considerable challenge to pilots trained to use the contours of the terrain. The task of aggressor pilots is also made easier by the fact that camouflage is of little use when a target aircraft is flying over a frozen lake. For the strike pilots, camouflaged sites among the trees and dummy tanks in clearings present difficult targets for an aircraft flying at 150 ft and 450 kt.

Broadly, the exercise pattern for Maple Flag follows that established for Red Flag, and begins with large numbers of aircraft carrying out attack, reconnaissance, combat air patrol, escort and defence suppression roles. At a later stage, participating aircraft are switched from Blue Force (attack and CAP) to Red Force (defensive) to give crews experience on both sides of the fence. Aircraft taking part in Maple Flag may include RAF Jaguars, Buccaneers or Tornados, which stage from the UK via Goose Bay, Bagotville, North Bay and Winnipeg, USAF F-5Es, F-15s, F-16s, F-4s, and Canadian Armed Forces CF-5s and CF-18 Hornets. Maple Flag also includes search and rescue missions; pilots designated as shot down are flown out to the range area to be picked up by fighter-escorted helicopters.

While the USAF's Tactical Fighter Weapons Centre at Nellis provides realistic combat training for Air Force crews, the US Navy has its own counterpart, the Fighter Weapons School at Miramar Naval Air Station, near San Diego in California. Known as Top Gun, it too had its roots in the Vietnam War; during the first five months of 1968, Navy pilots shot down nine MiGs while the enemy registered ten kills — a kill ratio acceptable only to the North Vietnamese. A later study showed that fifty air-to-air missiles were launched against attacking MiGs without destroying a single one, which was another unacceptable fact.

As a result, the Navy Air Systems Command appointed Captain Frank W. Ault to analyze aerial combat in South-East Asia. The reason for the poor showing against MiGs was obvious: swirling, low-altitude battles conducted visually in a gut-wrenching series of high-g manoeuvres. Keeping radar antennae trained on a darting enemy aircraft during a low-level, close-in encounter was like tracking a buzzing fly in a darkened room with a flashlight. The solution was also obvious; what was needed was improved missile reliability and more highly-skilled US fighter tactics.

Before the Ault report was even finished, Navy Air Systems Command recommended the formation of a graduate school to train a core of fighter crews for the fleet. The objective was to place

The two-seat Jaguar 'International B(0)' 1 pictured here in desert camouflage on a proving flight from Warton Aerodrome on 4 March 1977, prior to being handed over for service with the Sultan of Oman's Air Force.

at least one graduate in every Navy and Marine Corps squadron who would become highly competent in air combat manoeuvring and weapons deployment, a man who would then pass on his skills to the other squadron members.

VF-121, the Pacific Fleet replacement training squadron, was directed to establish a Navy Fighter Weapons School at NAS Miramar to coach F-4 crews, and the first class was accepted in March 1969. Top Gun became a commissioned unit in July 1972, with an average staff of seventeen instructors. The policy was, and still is, to select the best pilots and radar intercept officers from the Navy Fighter Weapons School and make instructors out of them.

In a typical exercise, Top Gun instructors loiter over the Arizona Desert in F-5E and A-4 aircraft as F-4 and F-14 crews attempt to locate them with radar. Then close-in 'hassling' begins with combinations of opponents ranging from one versus one, one versus two, two versus two, four versus two and four versus four. Various manoeuvres and formations are tested to provide the toughest problems possible. Towards the end of the course, trainees escort bombers on strike routes over the Pacific Ocean off Catalina Island. Somewhere along the route, Top Gun instructors pounce on the formation, testing the trainees' ability to kill the interceptors before the strike aircraft are shot down. The exercise usually involves an eight versus eight situation.

The five-week Top Gun course includes ninety hours of classroom work and thirty training sorties, each of which is followed by an hour or more of debriefing. Ground instruction consists of lectures, chalk-talks, slides and motion pictures of such subjects as conventional weapons, electronic warfare, air combat tactics, air-to-air gunnery and intelligence briefings on enemy aircraft and fighter performance.

One of the more important training aids, installed in the early 1970s, was a sophisticated device — part computer, part TV system — known as the Air Combat Manoeuvring Range (ACMR). The system covered a forty-mile range at altitudes of 5,000 to 50,000 ft and trained fighter pilots in dogfighting techniques. Every move made by the students in the air was monitored on a visual display unit, where it could be reviewed and analysed in replay after every mission.

The ACMR system comprised four major sub-systems. The Airborne Instrumentation Sub-system (AIS), mounted on a pod resembling a Sidewinder missile and adaptable to any aircraft capable of carrying the Sidewinder, measured aircraft and weapon performance during a dogfight and transmitted the information to ground facilities. The Tracking Instrumentation Sub-system (TIS), comprising six remote, solar-powered ground units, computed multiple ranges of up to sixteen aircraft simultaneously. The Computation and Control Sub-system (CCS) controlled the operation of the other sub-systems and performed complex computations with its Sigma-Five computers; it processed range, altitude and acceleration data transmitted from the aircraft,

Jaguar International of the Sultan of Oman's Air Force taking off on its delivery flight from Warton Aerodrome.

computed position, missile and flight simulations, and determined 'hits' or 'misses' for each participating aircraft. The Display and Debriefing Sub-system (DDS), located in three mobile vehicles, provided interactive graphic displays used to monitor all important facets of a mission; the entire exercise was controlled and operated from these master sites.

In July 1976 the US Air Force installed a more advanced version of ACMR, known as Air Combat Manoeuvring Instrumentation (ACMI), which today is used extensively in the Red Flag exercises. The US Navy followed suit, renaming its updated version the Tactical Aircrew Combat Training System (Tacts). ACMI/Tacts is, in fact, a total aircrew combat trainer; in addition to air-to-air combat training the system can now include air-to-ground and anti-radiation missiles, 'no-drop' bombing, 'no-drop' minelaying, drone control and electronic warfare threats.

When an aerial dogfight is in progress, those gathered before the monitoring screens can hear the short wave chatter that goes on continually between the instructor pilots and student pilots acting as aggressors. A two versus one situation, for example, might sound something like this:

Ground Controller	'Bogey...30° at 18 miles.'
Lead Aircraft	'Heading 340°, 17 miles.'
Wingman	'Visual.' (Meaning I see you.) 'Contact 20° right of nose.'
Lead Aircraft	'On nose, 6 miles.'

Four Jaguar International aircraft of the Sultan of Oman's Air Force on coastal patrol, armed with Sidewinder AAMs.

Wingman	'On nose at $2\frac{1}{2}$.'
Lead Aircraft	'Tally ho!'
Wingman	'Where is he?'
Lead Aircraft	'Passing...in a left-hand turn.'
Wingman	'Do you have a visual?'
Lead Aircraft	'Continue left turn and look a couple of thousand feet below the sun.'
Wingman	'Going hard left...got a visual.'
Lead Aircraft	'Fox Two.' (Simulated Sidewinder launch.)
Bogey	'OK...Good shot.'

In such dogfights, both instructors and students carry tape recorders that pick up all the chatter — even the grunts and groans produced by 6-g pullouts — and a kneeboard on which they write their impressions of the action as they return to base. As a Top Gun instructor explains,

'The object of debriefing is not for the purpose of an "I shot you down" ego trip, but the how and why. We try to be as objective as possible on what went right and what went wrong during a swirling dogfight that may have lasted only two or three minutes. And with three dogfights per flight, there's plenty to discuss. How many times did the student fire? How many times did he miss? More important, *why* did he miss? What did the enemy do to make his shot useless? What percentage of his range time was he in firing position? What percentage of the time was he vulnerable?'

One of the busiest ACMI installations is that owned by USAFE and sited at the Italian Air Force base at Decimomannu in Sardinia. The ACMI here became operational in 1979 for the training of NATO fast jet pilots and is primarily used by the USA and West Germany, who each provide 35 per cent of the funding for its support. The United Kingdom provides 20 per cent funding and Italy 10 per cent, figures which represent each country's range utilisation.

'Deci' is one of twelve such ranges throughout the world and is currently the only one in Europe. The range itself is a 30-nm diameter circle over the sea, about 50 nm off the west coast of Sardinia, with a base height of 5,000 ft and a ceiling of 50,000 ft. Any aircraft straying from the circle, unless in transit to and from the range, can be recalled to base by the local coastal radar at Mirto. This applies particularly to the adjacent north-west area outside the range, where there is a civilian air route.

The AIS pod carried by participating aircraft communicates directly with the ACMI's TCS sub-system; at Deci, this equipment is contained in four 35-ton buoys moored at sea beneath the range, one in the centre and the others around the circumference at 45°, 180° and 315°. Two additional unmanned land-based monitoring units, located on mountains to the north and south of Deci, complete the remote part of the TCS.

The information is passed to the land-based manned TCS master station situated some 4,000 ft up a mountain north of Deci and from there fed by microwave to the CCS at Deci. From the CCS computers, the data is passed to two 6 ft square graphical VDU screen displays above the Range Training Officer's (RTO) console and can be viewed by an audience of up to about twenty. Not only can the audience see the aircraft in plan view, but the image can be rotated through 90° to give an elevation. Further, a second screen which is normally utilised for an alpha-numeric display of the aircraft data can be used to show a graphical cockpit view of any selected combatant.

When an aircraft is 'killed', a coffin shape appears around it and the pilot is vectored out of the fight by his RTO for 45 seconds, at which point he is free to return and the coffin is removed. During this period the computer will not recognise, nor therefore record, any simulated missile launch or gun firing from the killed aircraft. The length of combat time over the range is strictly limited to twenty-minute slots.

To get an idea of the kind of combat training that goes on at Deci,

Flying very low and fast over the desert, a Jaguar International of the Sultan of Oman's Air Force pulls up in front of the camera. At low level, the small profile of the camouflaged Jaguar makes it a difficult target for CAP fighters.

let us follow the fortunes of a detachment of Sea Harriers of No 899 Headquarters and Training Naval Air Squadron that went there in June 1984. The prime task of the detachment was to provide air combat experience for two student pilots, Lieutenants Ted O'Connell and Tim Mannion, and priority was given to their sorties over all others.

During the first week, 899 acquired a back-up RTO in the form of Captain Dave Kuhn, USAF, from the 602nd Tactical Control Squadron based at Türkheim, West Germany. Captain Kuhn assisted 899's own RTO and Direction Officer, Lieutenant Tim Kelly, working alternative sorties, attending the briefings, taking charge of the ACMI control cabin during the combat and then running through the debrief with the pilots.

The 899 Squadron detachment comprised four Sea Harriers and two T8M Hunters, supported by eighty personnel. On this occasion they shared the facilities at Decimomannu with the Jaguars of Nos 14 and 17 Squadrons RAF, which had flown down from Bruggen to use the air/ground ranges at Cape Frasca. The Sea Harrier detachment was led by 899's Commanding Officer, Lieutenant-

Commander Denis Thornton; by the end of the first week he professed himself content with the progress of the student training programme and opened negotiations with the USAF for a sortie against F-5s and F-15s in a 'two versus two versus two', although as one might expect it ended up as a 'two plus two versus two'.

In this first sortie against foreign nationals, the two Sea Harriers involved were flown by Lieutenant Commander Thornton and Lieutenant Dave Morgan and had the respective callsigns of Bentley 1 and 2. The F-5s were provided by the 527th Tactical Fighter Training Aggressor Squadron from Alconbury in the UK, and the F-15s by the 32nd Tactical Fighter Squadron from Germany.

The twenty-minute sortie showed the vast difference between the US and UK tactics and roles. Both US types remained at high level in the initial stages where their higher performance could be used to effect, with the F-5s loitering at 35,000 ft and the F-15s at 40,000, watching the fight developing beneath them. At first the Sea Harriers were pitted against the F-5s only, but within minutes of combat being joined the F-5s were beginning to run out of fuel due to their being configured without drop tanks and the necessity for them to use afterburners almost constantly in order to extricate themselves from threatening situations.

With the F-5s out of the fight, the stage was clear for the Sea Harriers to tackle the F-15s. Combat was still at high level, although one of the F-15s tended to get much lower than its partner and 'mix it'. Unsupported by his consort, the result was almost a foregone conclusion. He was hit repeatedly, and on one occasion his wingman actually left the confines of the range, leaving the leader alone.

The debrief between the six pilots was interesting in that it revealed the techniques and intentions adopted by the pairs. The F-5s' approach was to remain at medium to high level to try and draw the Sea Harriers up to them, while the F-15s had intended to fight on the climb-and-drive, swooping down occasionally to pick off a target before returning to high level to repeat the tactics. The Sea Harriers, on the other hand, attempted to draw down the opposition to low or medium level, where their pilots could use the Harrier's unique combination of rapid deceleration and violent evasive manouevring to best advantage.

The second Monday of the detachment brought with it a repeat of Friday's 'two versus two versus two' sortie with the USAF

An RF-4C Phantom of the 10th TRW accompanied by two F-5E Tigers of the 527th Aggressor Squadron. Similar in profile to the MiG-21, these aircraft provide realistic combat training.

squadrons. Each had learned from the previous Friday's combat, and the day saw a reversal of tactics: this time the F-15s came in at about 7,000 ft while the Sea Harriers were up at 20,000 ft, with the F-5s about half-way between the two formations. The Sea Harriers, flown by Squadron Leader Neil Matheson, RAF, and Lieutenant Commander Mike Watson, managed to stay together as a pair for the bulk of the time and repeatedly proved the effectiveness of a pair working in unison, finishing the exercise with a high score.

Later that morning another joint exercise took place, this time with a pair of Sea Harriers versus a pair of F-15s. One of the F-15s went u/s prior to take-off, but his partner decided to carry on alone. On this sortie there was a requirement to prove the intercept geometry required for a beam shot against a supersonic target, so the lone F-15, flown by Captain Davies, USAF, went to the north of the range, turned and headed for the Sea Harriers, increasing speed to 1.9M at 26,000 ft. Lieutenant Simon Hargreaves and Lieutenant Morgan were tasked with this interception, and as the

F-15 closed with them they turned in to fire and brought the engagement to a successful conclusion.

When the Sea Harriers returned to Deci in close formation with the F-15 the sheer size of the US aircraft was apparent; it was by no means difficult to see at long range. On the other hand, F-15 pilots admitted to having considerable difficulty in picking out the Harrier because of the latter's relatively small size. To quote one of them: 'I was up at 35,000 ft and when I looked down I had great trouble in seeing you guys. When I did, you looked like a couple of bugs.'

Thursday of that week saw the first Sea Harrier sortie against Luftwaffe F-4 Phantoms, plus the arrival of four F-14 Tomcats from the nuclear-powered attack carrier USS *Saratoga*. The Luftwaffe proved to be very competent and professional in their approach, with tactics involving a pincer attack manoeuvre which turned out to be very effective. The first sortie was disappointing for 899, but the second showed great improvement with the Sea Harriers splitting up the F-4s before picking them off. The Germans tended to enter combat flying parallel, but with one aircraft 2,000–3,000 ft higher than his consort. Allowing the Sea Harriers to pass between them, the F-4s would turn inwards simultaneously, giving them a choice of which target to pick off. However, the Sea Harriers managed to keep them apart during subsequent sorties and out-manoeuvre them, preventing them from acting as a pair.

Like any NATO squadron that uses Deci, No 899 went away a much sharper and more capable unit than when it first arrived. The two novice pilots in particular had found it an invaluable experience to see the fight from their attackers' point of view on the RTO's display screens, assessing any mistakes they themselves had made through their opponents' eyes. Like others using the ACMI system, they had learned in a fortnight what it used to take junior pilots several months to learn.

And, as the pilots of both the Royal Navy and Royal Air Force found when they were pitched into the Falklands War in May 1982, the time available for an operational squadron to prepare for action may be measured in days, rather than weeks.

Chapter 2
The Harrier: NATO's cavalry

'May the Force be with you' is a saying they have at RAF Gutersloh in Germany. The station is right in the potential front line — only seventy miles from the East German border — and the force referred to is the Harrier Force. It is not large, comprising the 36 Harriers of Nos 3 and 4 Squadrons, but Gutersloh's position in the centre of the British NATO defence zone within the Northern Army Group (NORTHAG) allows the Harriers to cover the 1st British Corps as well as the Dutch, German and Belgian Corps in the NORTHAG AREA. The presence of the Harriers, which in time of emergency would be reinforced by a further twelve aircraft of No 233 Operational Conversion Unit at Wittering in the United Kingdom, is of vital importance, for Gutersloh lies in the path of what could be a principal axis of any major Soviet move against the West.

The key elements in Harrier operations are mobility, flexibility, surprise and rapid response — requirements which, in the past, were met by cavalry formations and more recently, in Vietnam, by helicopters. Today's Harrier squadrons operate off-base from sites hidden along the fringes of the forests in Germany, ready for launch as an attack/reconnaissance force against the enemy and afterwards returning to cover to prepare for the next sortie. The Harrier's ability to take off and land independently of fixed runways makes it a force-multiplier out of all proportion to the relatively small number of aircraft deployed.

At Gutersloh itself, the Harriers are housed in reinforced concrete shelters which were originally designed and built for the Lightnings of Nos 19 and 92 Squadrons; these operated from Gutersloh in the air defence role until the late 1970s. In the event of hostilities, it can be readily assumed that the vulnerable runways and taxiways would sustain serious damage despite heavy attrition against the

A Harrier GR 1 of No 3 Squadron waits for a 20 Squadron Harrier to land during Exercise Grim Charade, held in Nordrhein-Westphalen in 1973.

enemy by the Rapier SAM units that defend the airfield; one or two runway denial missiles would be sufficient to put an airfield and its complement of conventional aircraft out of action, and because of the large base area involved it is impossible to defend an airfield adequately, either with guns or SAMs. It must not be assumed, either, that an airfield strike would be carried out by low flying aircraft; short-range surface-to-surface missiles, which nowadays are highly accurate, might be used instead, and against these there is no defence.

Without doubt, a high proportion of NATO's combat aircraft in Germany would be able to get off the ground before their airfields were hit. But how and where would they recover? Instant concrete has to be really quick-setting to fill holes that appear when the squadrons are airborne. If there is no intact diversionary airfield available to the pilot of a conventional aircraft once his mission is completed, he is faced with three alternatives. Either he lands on a designated stretch of autobahn, or he makes a forced landing on a damaged airfield, or he ejects.

The name of the game, therefore, is to get off the base and to seek protection through dispersal and concealment, and the only aircraft in NATO's armoury that can at present be deployed in such a manner — operating from dispersed and remote locations, requiring very little support and take-off run — is the Harrier. Of all fixed-wing jet aircraft, it alone provides these tactical benefits of mobility, flexibility, surprise and rapid response: keeping the enemy guessing, invalidating his intelligence and dissipating his resources.

Under any anticipated scenario, NATO forces would have a considerable period of time to prepare — probably several weeks during which the signs of impending offensive moves would become apparent. Today, intelligence gathering has reached such a pitch of technological perfection that a major surprise attack by either side would be an impossibility.

As the political tension increases, the Warsaw Pact forces would have to gather and deploy along the eastern border and then dismantle their own anti-tank emplacements and fixed defences to allow clear passage for their armoured columns. As soon as this build-up was detected, the RAF would begin the movement of its own forces to sites in the field, first despatching the helicopter units and then the Harrier squadrons. At this point, the Station Commander of Gutersloh relinquishes his command of that station and becomes strictly the commander of the Harrier Force. Gutersloh would then assume its wartime role as a major reinforcement airfield — for as long as its runways remained intact. In this role, it would be able to receive and disseminate thousands of troops within a matter of hours, unloading two widebodied

An early Harrier GR 1 on a low-level sortie from RAF Wittering.

aircraft simultaneously with a turnround time of less than an hour.

From their main base, the Harriers would deploy to locations roughly triangulated around the central command post, each site containing six to eight aircraft. The whereabouts of the dispersal sites to be used in the event of war are naturally secret, although all of them are near hard surfaces so that it is not necessary to lay down steel take-off and landing areas. (This, in fact, is standard practice during peacetime manoeuvres.) The Harrier Force could either activate old training sites or move into pre-selected rural sites in the vicinity of woods, barns or old farmhouses; if war is declared, the options would be increased to include urban areas.

Once in the field, the Harrier Force Headquarters comprise the personnel responsible for air operations, engineering and logistics, ground defence operations and intelligence. The trailers which house the HQ personnel are filtered and pressurized to allow safe operation in the event of a nuclear, biological or chemical attack. The Harrier Force deployment sites are secured and protected by Nos 1 and 2 Squadrons, RAF Regiment; these light armoured-car squadrons are trained to secure the area on the ground and are equipped with Scorpion and Spartan tracked combat recon-naissance vehicles. The Harriers themselves are concealed in camouflaged hides and are virtually invisible to all but infra-red detection.

From these hidden sites, the Harrier Force operates using STO (Short Take-Off) launches to permit increased fuel and weapons payload for the sortie, and VL (Vertical Landing) to reduce taxi-ing and 'push-back' time on return. There is a saying among V/STOL pilots that it is safer to stop and then land than land and then hope to stop.

In the field, each hide is self-contained and the aircraft can be refuelled, re-armed and ready to go within thirty minutes. To reduce turnround time, pilots remain in their cockpits during this period to receive their briefings for the next sortie by landline. The turnround itself could be even further reduced, but is kept to thirty minutes to reduce stress and fatigue among the ground crews. On a peacetime RAF station, a typical sortie rate is three in a five-hour period. The Harrier, however, has such a rapid turnround time that with a typical thirty-minute sortie and a thirty-minute turnround, the squadrons can perform one sortie per hour per aircraft. This rate provides for eight sorties per day per aircraft and over 200 sorties per day from the total Harrier Force, even when maintenance down-time is taken into consideration. Pilots normally fly from five to six sorties per day, broken into groups of two or three.

An example of the high sortie rate that can be achieved was provided during NATO's Exercise Crusader '80, when 28 Harriers flew a total of 1,120 sorties in a nine-day period. In another exercise in the United Kingdom Harriers flew an average of ten sorties per day over a three-day period, and in Exercise Lionheart, held in September 1984, the two Harrier squadrons in Germany notched up 120 sorties in four hours, operating from five field sites.

The rule of thumb for Harrier operations from dispersed sites is that if you can drive a Land Rover over a site without breaking anything, you can operate Harriers from it. The problem most often encountered, in fact, is that of pilots overshooting the site on returning from a sortie because the sites are so expertly camouflaged. Harrier pilots are sceptical at the prospect of conventional aircraft operating from roads without continuous training for the role, as in Sweden. As one of them put it: 'Taking off from a road in a conventional aircraft is OK. You line up, psyche up and blast off. Landing is a different matter. At 130 kt or more you will need a big chunk of road. Frankly, a real star might get it right but your average squadron pilot will probably say "no thanks" and divert.'

The Harrier's ability to accept exacting operational demands was well demonstrated during the Falklands War in the summer of 1982. Soon after the establishment of the San Carlos beachhead, the Royal Engineers constructed a forward operating base on a site on the north shore of San Carlos water. This consisted of a 1,200 ft aluminium matting (Mexe) strip with parking and holding loops at one end. It was provided with a refuelling capability by using standard 'pillow' tanks of the type used at dispersed sites in Germany, and these were regularly topped up by floating tanks which plied between tankers stationed in San Carlos water. The base could accommodate up to nine Harriers, and more than 150 Harrier refuellings were completed during the brief campaign.

Harriers flying from the carrier task force well to the east of the islands took up stations over the land on Combat Air Patrol (Sea Harriers) or airborne support stations behind the land force lines (Harrier GR 3s) until their fuel state ran down. If the aircraft were serviceable and weapons were unexpended, the Harriers would land at the forward operating base and refuel. The Sea Harriers

A Harrier GR 3 refuelling from a Victor K 2 tanker of No 57 Squadron. Flight refuelling enabled the RN/RAF Harrier force to be rapidly reinforced during the Falklands War.

were launched again on patrol and afterwards returned to their ships after fuel depletion or combat.

The GR 3s on the ground at the forward operating base awaited a tasking call from the land forces. When this was received, the pair of pilots would plan the sortie in their cockpits, start up and take off. Typically, they would arrive in the target area in about twenty minutes of the task being set. Afterwards, they would return to the carriers for replenishment and rearming. On one occasion, when a helicopter had damaged part of the forward operating base's metal matting, Harriers landed vertically to refuel on the aft platforms of the RN assault ships *Fearless* and *Intrepid*, which were nearby.

Including training and CAP sorties flown during the passage south from Ascension Island the Harriers flew more than 2,000 missions, 1,650 within the Falklands Total Exclusion Zone. This translated into a flying rate of approximately 55 hours per aircraft per month, up to six sorties per aircraft per day and three to four sorties per day per pilot, involving up to ten hours in the cockpit.

Initially the task force had an average of 1.2 pilots for each aircraft and this was later increased to an average of 1.4. Overall Harrier availability was over 95 per cent, and only 1 per cent of planned sorties were cancelled due to unserviceability.

In one classic incident, a Harrier GR 3 of No 1 Squadron flown by Flight Lieutenant Murdo Macleod was hit by a single bullet during a ground attack sortie on 12 June 1982, passing rearwards and upwards through the rear Reaction Control System (RCS) which provides control when the aircraft is in the hover. Macleod recovered to HMS *Hermes*, unaware of the damage, but when he decelerated for vertical landing with the nozzles down the RCS was pressurized by high-pressure — and high-temperature — bleed air; this deflected a 350°C stream of air on to the inside of the rear fuselage, which started smoking and shedding large flakes of blistered paint. Macleod made an immaculate vertical landing and made a quick exit from the aircraft while the fire crew covered the rear fuselage with foam. By this time, the rear fuselage was cooking nicely and a lot of paint had been burnt off or was smouldering, in some cases right down to the bare metal. In addition, several items of equipment and electrical wiring in the rear compartment were burnt out. Nevertheless, the Harrier was out of action for only 36 hours and suffered no permanent damage.

On its dispersal sites in Germany, one of the Harrier's biggest assets is the secure communications that exist throughout the entire system. When minutes can mean the difference between victory or defeat, commands can be transmitted from the site operations centres direct to the pilot sitting in the cockpit, ready for immediate launch. Direct communication to the pilot is normally via a secure line to the site operations room. Mission assignments are received by the Force HQ direct from the Air Support Operations Centre (ASOC) at 1st British Corps Headquarters via a secure communications link.

The system gives the Harrier Force a response time of only tens of minutes rather than the hour or so it would normally take, and it is response time that is the key to successful battlefield ground-attack support. Experience by the United States Marine Corps during the Vietnam War proved that air support with conventional aircraft flying from a main base many miles to the rear of the front line, or from an aircraft carrier some miles off the coast, could mean an unacceptable reaction delay of forty to sixty minutes. In modern warfare, speed of movement and rapidly changing local tactical fortunes could mean that the aircraft delivers too much ordnance too late — or, even worse, the ordnance could fall on a friendly unit that had moved into the area during reaction delay time. There were many such tragic instances in the Second World War, the Korean War, and in the limited wars before Vietnam.

In spite of the relatively long warning time that is to be expected before any outbreak of hostilities in Europe, any Warsaw Pact invasion across the East German border would be sudden and massive, with aircraft and missile attacks designed to knock out NATO airfields followed by massed columns of tanks supported by other armoured fighting vehicles and infantry. In the event of such an onslaught, the role of the Harrier Force will be mass attacks against large concentrations of enemy forces — a tank column, for example, caught in a bottleneck or crossing a river.

Under such conditions the Harriers might be tasked to work in conjunction with RAF Jaguars, USAF A-10s, Luftwaffe Alpha Jets, Belgian Mirages or Dutch F-16s to destroy tank columns while RAF and Luftwaffe Tornados would attack enemy airfields and other strategic points in the rear of the enemy advance. RAF Phantoms and Tornado ADVs, USAF F-111s, F-15s and F-16s, flown by US, Belgian and Dutch pilots, would provide top cover to gain and hold air superiority.

When not tasked with mass attacks, the Harrier Force would operate in small groups, scouting enemy movements, hitting small convoys and troop concentrations or supporting ground forces in contact with the enemy. To assist the pilot to carry out these various tasks, the Harrier is equipped with the Ferranti FE 541 Inertial Navigation and Attack System (INAS), which is totally independant of external radio aids. INAS comprises a Sperry C2G compass, Smiths Industries electronic head-up display of flight information, Smiths air data computer and a Marconi ARI 18223 rear warning radar receiver. It can be aligned equally well over land or sea.

The weapon-aiming computer provides a general solution for manual or automatic release of free-fall and retarded bombs and for the aiming of rockets and guns in diving and straight-pass attacks over a wide range of flight conditions and very considerable freedom of manoeuvre in elevation. The pilot sets the co-ordinates of his own position and that of the reported target, then uses INAS to direct him to the ordnance release point. If a target of opportunity is spotted en route to the primary target, the pilot calls

Harrier GR 3s of No 3 Squadron carrying practice bomb dispensers.

up the former on INAS and receives range and heading for a secondary engagement, assuming of course that he has enough ordnance left.

The Harrier GR 3 is fitted with the Ferranti Type 106 Laser Ranger and Marked Target Seeker (LRMTS), which was used to good effect in the latter stages of the Falklands campaign when Harriers were tasked with attacking targets in the vicinity of Port Stanley using 1,000 lb Paveway laser-guided bombs — the first operational example of this type of attack. The bombs were dropped by the Harriers in a LOFT release, similar in principle to an underarm throw, about 6–7 km away from the target. While the aircraft turned away, the bombs rose through a trajectory of 30° to peak at 1,500 ft before falling towards the target. As the bomb descended, the target was illuminated by a ground mounted Ferranti Laser Designator and the weapon locked on to the laser light reflected from the target.

The Harrier GR 3 carries an F.95 oblique camera which shoots through an optically flat panel in the port side of the nose and which is supplemented by a cockpit voice recorder with in-flight playback facility; this is valuable for rapid debriefing and mission evaluation. The aircraft's ordnance is carried on four underwing and one under-fuselage release points fitted with ML ejector release units. The Harrier has no built-in armament, but it carries twin 30 mm Aden gun pods with a total of 300 rounds of ammunition. Typical ordnance combinations would be six underwing 68 mm or 2-in Matra Type 116M or 115 multiple rocket launchers; up to five 1,000 lb free-fall or retarded bombs; up to five BL-755 cluster bombs; up to ten Lepus flares; one centreline store and two underwing 100 gal combat tanks; or two 330 gal ferry tanks. The combinations can be varied up to a maximum ordnance load of 5,000 lb, although the aircraft has flown with a weapon load of 3,000 lb.

The pilot of the Harrier GR 3 sits on a Martin Baker Mk 9D zero-zero rocket ejection seat which is activated by pulling upwards on the single firing handle, situated in front of the seat pan. The seat is fitted with canopy breakers and the canopy itself is equipped with a miniature detonating cord for safe fragmentation when the seat goes through. The rocket burn lasts for 0.4 seconds and boosts the seat and its occupant to 130 mph from zero-zero activation; peak trajectory is 400 ft. Drogue stablization of the seat, deployment of the pilot's parachute and separation from the seat operate in the normal manner thereafter.

The all-important head-up display is mounted at the top of the cockpit's centre console so that the display coincides with the pilot's eye level. By means of a cathode-ray tube and reflector glass, the unit shows all information relevant to the flight — navigational data, target co-ordinates, instrument data, weapon aiming and release data and so on. Directly below the HUD on the centre console is the projected moving map display provided by INAS.

The port instrument panel contains conventional instruments whose inputs are separate from the HUD system, and which therefore provide a standby flight information system for cross-checking. The lower part of the port console contains the undercarriage main and emergency controls, the undercarriage position indicator, flap selector and indicator. Also on the port instrument panel are the armament selector and jettison switches.

The engine and fuel instruments are located on the starboard panel, above the nav-attack switches. The starboard console contains the compass repeater and the switches and muters for the Plessey U/VHF, Ultra standby UHF, Cossor IFF and other communications equipment. The lower section of the starboard panel incorporates the GEC Avionics AD2770 Tacan indicator.

The combined engine throttle and nozzle control box, which is mounted on the port console, is a clever piece of engineering and is so designed that the pilot can operate it without having to look down at it. The one box incorporates the throttle lever, which controls the engine speed and the length of the thrust vector, the nozzle lever, controlling the direction of the thrust vector, an adjustable short take-off stop, a fixed vertical take-off stop, a parking brake lock and a limiter-off switch. The throttle lever handle has a twist-grip control for weapon aiming, and also incorporates the engine re-light button, airbrake switch and radio transmit switch.

For vertical take-off and subsequent transition to forward flight, the Harrier pilot first of all lines up the aircraft, using the steerable nosewheel, and applies the brakes. He then moves the nozzle lever to Hover Stop and opens the throttle to full power, upon which the aircraft lifts off. Two or three seconds later, with the Harrier safely airborne, the pilot retracts the undercarriage. The throttle is then used for height control and normal movements of the control column and rudder pedals control attitude and heading by means of the Reaction Control System. At about 50 ft, when the aircraft is clear of ground effect, the pilot selects flaps IN and moves the nozzle lever steadily forward, rotating the nozzles aft to hold height. From VTO to fully wingborne flight at around 180 kt takes less than twenty seconds and requires less than 100 lb of fuel.

In short take-off mode, where the wing provides extra lift for fuel and weapon loads, the pilot once again lines up the aircraft and

The two-seat Harrier T 2 taking off on a flight from Dunsfold.

applies the brakes, at the same time setting a notch on the ASI to lift-off speed. He then sets the nozzle stop to 50° and opens the throttle to 55 per cent RPM. When this is indicated he releases the brakes and slams open the throttle to full power. At lift-off speed he moves the nozzle lever to the stop, rotating the nozzles to an intermediate setting and the aircraft becomes airborne on a combination of wing lift and engine thrust. At 50 ft he selects flaps IN, moves the nozzle lever forward to hold height, and at 180 kt the aircraft is fully wingborne. In this mode, with a 5,000 lb payload at maximum take-off weight, the Harrier will lift off in about 1,000 ft. Both the length of the take-off run and the wind speed contribute to the extra lift from the wing in the STO mode; over 6 lb additional load can be carried per foot of run and/or some 66 lb of extra load for each knot of wind speed.

Returning from a sortie for a vertical landing, the pilot first of all carries out his normal landing checks and selects flaps and undercarriage down. Downwind from the landing site, he selects the nozzles to 20° to check the reaction system. The Harrier has normal aerodynamic controls (tailplane, ailerons and rudder) but in the hover and at very low IAS these are ineffective, so control is maintained through the Reaction Control System (RCS) mentioned earlier in this chapter. High-pressure air, taken from the engine, is ducted to reaction control valves (RCVs) at the nose, tail and wingtips. The RCVs have shutters which are mechanically connected to their associated aerodynamic controls. They produce air jets which exert a reaction force on the aircraft in the natural sense demanded by the pilot — in other words a backward pressure on the control column opens the nose RCV, producing a downward jet and an upward reaction force to raise the nose.

On final approach, the pilot selects a nozzle angle of 40° and uses the throttle to maintain an angle of attack of 8–9°. At a height of 50 ft and a distance of 1,200 yd from the hover point, he moves the nozzle lever to Hover Stop and uses the throttle to maintain the flight path as the speed reduces. Fine adjustments of the control column are used to position the aircraft over the hover point at 50 ft. When this is attained the pilot uses the throttle very sensitively to reduce the RPM by one or two per cent, establishing a slow descent while maintaining position and attitude with the control column. As soon as the undercarriage contacts the ground firmly the pilot closes the throttle to engine idling RPM, then selects the nozzles fully aft and applies the brakes.

The Harrier's Rolls-Royce Pegasus Mk 103 vectored thrust turbofan engine has two compressor turbine systems which contra-rotate on concentric shafts, giving added aircraft stability. It develops up to 21,500 lb static thrust at sea level by moving a large mass of air at relatively low velocity and temperature, so that jet blast effects near the ground are minimal. Fuel consumption is low; the maximum at full throttle at low altitude is about 220 lb per minute, and in the hover, before a vertical landing, 180 lb per minute. Compare this with, for example, the fuel consumption of an F-4 Phantom at take-off — 1,200 lb per minute.

The Pegasus engine's combination of high thrust and low fuel consumption, together with the fact that it does not use reheat, allows the Harrier to stay in combat until an enemy aircraft is forced to disengage because of fuel shortage, at which point it immediately becomes vulnerable. Another good point about the Pegasus in combat is that it produces hardly any smoke, and smoke-trails, as we saw in chapter one, are a big giveaway.

The Harrier pilot can deflect the engine thrust when in combat by simply operating the nozzle lever. This vectoring in forward flight (VIFF) gives additional manoeuvring capability, with large attitude changes and rapid speed variations, and was in fact developed as a combat manoeuvring procedure by the United States Marine Corps with their own brand of Harrier, the AV-8A. Combat trials showed that, using VIFF, a Harrier/AV-8A was capable of holding its own against, and in many cases getting the upper hand over, much 'hotter' aircraft like the F-14, F-15 and F-18.

Despite much speculation in the Press at the time, VIFF was never used in the Falklands War, where the Royal Navy's Sea Harriers convincingly demonstrated the type's value as a fighter aircraft. This was partly because there were no air-to-air combats as such between the Sea Harriers and their Argentinian opponents; it was a matter of 'pursue and destroy' as the Argentine jets went all out for the vessels of the task force. But in any case, many RAF and Royal Navy pilots have mixed feelings about the value of VIFF, which has its disadvantages.

VIFF is useful if the Harrier itself is being attacked; used in conjunction with violent evasive action it enables the aircraft to decelerate very quickly, presenting an attacking aircraft with a difficult shot with either cannon or missiles. Apart from that, VIFF can be valuable in enabling the pilot to pull the nose of his aircraft round or up a few extra degrees that might be necessary to get off a

The Sea Harrier FRS Mk 1, the aircraft without which Britain could not have retaken the Falklands Islands in 1982. The Sea Harrier's low-visibility camouflage, small profile and smoke-free exhaust make it an extremely difficult aircraft to spot, and its ability to vector in forward flight can often give it the edge in air combat manoeuvring.

shot — but he has to get it right first time, otherwise the target aircraft will rapidly move out of range as a result of the Harrier's sudden deceleration. In any case, rapid deceleration in the middle of a combat can be dangerous; it might enable a Harrier pilot to evade one attacking fighter, but he then risks being shot down by the latter's wingman.

The Royal Navy's Sea Harriers in the Falklands owed their success to two principal factors. First, the Sea Harrier's small size and grey camouflage made them very difficult to spot, with the result that they almost invariably saw the enemy first — an aspect aided by the aircraft's nose-mounted Blue Fox multi-mode radar and the raised cockpit, which affords excellent all-round visibility; and the second factor was the AIM-9L Sidewinder air-to-air missile, carried as standard armament on the Sea Harrier. Twenty-six Sidewinders were fired by Sea Harriers during the conflict — mostly in the course of engagements at between 50 and 500 ft, involving high load factor manoeuvring at speeds of around 550 kt — and of these nineteen resulted in kills, a success rate of 82 per cent.

Although the Harrier was a British concept, it was one that would never have been developed without the injection of substantial American funding. American interest in the V/STOL concept was maintained throughout the 1960s, and although the USAF and US Navy would not commit themselves, the United States Marine Corps came down firmly on the side of the idea. It was Vietnam, a land war requiring timely, fixed wing close air support, that tipped the scales in the Harrier's favour, and the aircraft was ordered into production for the USMC as the AV-8A.

Although the AV-8A's service debut came too late for it to see action in Vietnam, the Marines were soon convinced that the concept was right. In the words of one senior USMC officer, Colonel Harry Blot:

'We could not afford, both in terms of initial cost or the impact on logistics to buy enough [conventional] airplanes to keep them in the air all the time waiting to be called. We had to look for something we could park closer to the front lines. The Harrier seemed to be the answer, so we purchased three squadrons to prove the concept. The more we tested it, the more we knew it would work. Though the AV-8A was limited, we could clearly see the potential. The only reason the Marines own airplanes is to support the guy with the rifle and everything is wrapped around that mission.'

The first US Marine Corps TAV-8A (Harrier T Mk 54) pictured flying from Dunsfold in 1975.

Although the AV-8A Harrier was conceptually correct, the Marines needed an aircraft with more capacity. As a result, the AV-8B Harrier II programme was launched. Although the design leadership of the advanced Harrier rested with McDonnell Douglas, it soon developed into a joint effort between that company and British Aerospace in the ratio of sixty:forty; today it represents the biggest Euro-American collaborative aircraft programme in history, valued at about $16 billion.

The AV-8B, alias Harrier GR 5 to the Royal Air Force, is a vastly different aircraft from the original Harrier. The wing has increased area and reduced sweepback to improve longitudinal stability at high angles of attack, such as when stores are being carried, and the increased internal fuel tankage has raised the number of underwing weapon pylons from four to six. Wing lift during take-off is augmented by a large trailing edge single-slotted flap which is linked to nozzle deflection and induces airflow over the wing; the rear nozzle efflux directs air over the deflected flap, increasing the velocity and therefore the pressure differential between the upper and lower surfaces. In the short take-off mode, this generates over 6,700 lb additional lift. In addition, composite materials have been used extensively to save weight. Carbon-fibre material is also used in the tailplane structure.

The Harrier II's performance is boosted by under-fuselage Lift Improvement Devices (LIDS), improved air intakes, Leading Edge

Sea Harrier FRS Mk 51s in the markings of the Indian Navy, which operates six of these aircraft as well as two T Mk 60s.

Root Extensions (LERX) and an enhanced version of the Pegasus engine. The avionics have been substantially updated and include the Hughes angle-rate bombing system (ARBS), which comprises a laser/TV tracker in the nose to provide all-weather launch capability not only for laser-guided weapons but also for iron bombs and Maverick TV-guided ASMs. The avionics also include an AYK-14 mission computer of the type used in the F-18 Hornet. Other main avionics equipment comprises an ASN-130 inertial navigation system — also used in the F-18 — TACAN, radar beacon and radar altimeter, an all-weather approach and landing system, ALR-67 radar warning receiver, ALE-39 flare and chaff dispenser, and a podded jamming system known as ASPJ.

The Harrier II is fitted with the HOTAS (Hands on Throttle and Stick) system, which is described by Colonel Harry Blot:

'In the earlier AV-8A we had 1960s switchology. In combat we found that, across the board, what was acceptable in peacetime was no longer acceptable in wartime. You are trying to fight another airplane and you have a lot of 'g' on you. In the AV-8A you must look and reach to throw a switch, then turn round again. You just can't do that when someone is trying to kill you. You don't want to take your eyes off him.'

'Now in the AV-8B we have a system that will allow you, without letting go of either throttle or stick, to switch from an offensive to defensive mode without ever taking your eyes away from the enemy.' (The system, in fact, comprises all engine and flight controls except the rudder, radar warning control, ARBS/TV slew control, armament selector, gun trigger and bomb release, Sidewinder target designator and lock-on and manoeuvring flap switch.)

'So if I'm running in on target to destroy it and I'm being attacked, then with one flick of the thumb the Harrier II system completely changes all my sensors, arms my air-to-air weapons, changes my displays, head up and head down, and I am totally prepared for air combat. If the attacker doesn't turn in, then one more flick of my thumb and the aircraft goes back to being optimized for air-to-ground. In wartime, that's absolutely vital.'

First deliveries of the AV-8B were made in January 1984 to Training Squadron VMAT-203 at Marine Corps Air Station Cherry Point, North Carolina, which undertook pilot conversion prior to the formation of the first AV-8B squadron, VMA-331, at the same location. Weapons qualification and sea trials are carried out from

The Sea Harrier cockpit layout. Compare this with the advanced layout and equipment of the Harrier GR 5 (AV-8B, Harrier II) below.

Naval Air Station Patuxent River, which is the US Navy's Air Test Centre. Pilots are completely enthusiastic about the Harrier II's performance.

According to them, one of the biggest refinements is the OBOGS — On-Board Oxygen Generating System, which one veteran pilot described as the biggest advance since he started flying. With the AV-8A, trans-Pacific deployments were limited by the amount of oxygen carried; the system in the Harrier II enables the aircraft to stay airborne as long as there are tankers available to refuel it.

Pilots are also highly impressed by the Angle-Rate Bombing System, which is claimed to make the AV-8B the most accurate air-to-ground weapons platform ever developed by the US Navy, used in conjunction with the INS computer. The latter gives the pilot what has been described as God's eye view on the world, with him in the centre. The Digital Data Indicator gives him his best cruise profile, best altitude for range, Tacan, INS information, time to go, distance to go, engine data and what is on the weapon pylons, along with laser and ALQ-162 information. (The ALQ-162 is a 35-lb ECM pack developed by Northrop for use in smaller US Navy combat aircraft.) The pilot can also transfer HUD information on to the DDI if the HUD goes unserviceable.

The INS is extremely accurate, and used properly will bring up the Initial Point 'bang on the nose'. Lieutenant-Colonel Jimmy Cranford, officer commanding VMA-331 on its conversion to the AV-8B, says:

'The ARBS is outstanding. On an A-4 or F-4 squadron the old hands will achieve a CEP [Circular Error Probable — a measure of the accuracy attributable to ballistic weapons] of about 50 ft and the young guys will turn in 70–75 ft, something like that. And that's range work; in real life you've got SAMs, AAA, bad guys to contend with. With the AV-8B I can use terrain masking to run in low. My accurate INS puts me on the IP, I pull up and zoom, say to attack a SAM site, up high, roll in, drop on the SAMs before I get in AAA range, then beat feet out of there. And do you know what's really nice? I won't have to go back and do it again tomorrow because I missed — that *is* nice. All the time I'm in that attack the system is working for me.'

'I don't need to worry about airspeed, wind velocity, angle of dive or all that old stuff. I can use my guns and drop my bombs at the same time, give the guys shooting at *me* a hard time; that's nice, too! This aeroplane and ARBS puts the bomb exactly where you lock it; now if that isn't where the target is that's *your* fault. My worst bomb was a 150 ft miss on a LOFT attack because *I* screwed up. When I don't, this sucker can loft in a 20 ft bomb from three miles out.'

The same pilot adds that compared with the AV-8A, it's all up except the workload. 'Range up, payload up, accuracy up, manoeuvrability up, workload down. When we were out at Yuma we were fragged to do a wing escort of a helicopter formation, with us and a bunch of AV-8As flying a top cover weave over these CH-53s and stuff. Real fuel-thirsty work. Well, after about 45 minutes the As bingoed out for fuel and I had another fifteen to twenty minutes on station, easily.'

In air combat situations, Harrier II pilots will need to use VIFF only as a last resort; the new wing and the leading edge root extensions enable the aircraft to out-turn or at least match conventional types such as the F-15 — and that includes the Su-27 Flanker and MiG-29 Fulcrum, the Soviet Union's latest air superiority fighters in the F-15 and F-16 class. If a Harrier II pilot gets into difficulties in a turning fight he can either use VIFF or flap, in which case nothing except another V/STOL fighter will match him. He is aided, too, by the excellent all-round visibility provided by the raised cockpit, which enables him to see down below, over the nose, and the six o'clock area without having to strain.

The extra engine power and the aircraft's Stability Augmentation System combine to make the Harrier II a much easier machine to land than its predecessor, which begins to lose wing lift at about 90 kt as it approaches its site for a vertical landing. The pilot of the Harrier II, on the other hand, can fly his aircraft down to 50 kt with 60° of nozzle, and the Stability Augmentation System cuts out all the 'wobble' that has hitherto resulted from over-sensitive stick movements.

All in all, the AV-8B/Harrier GR 5 promises to be one of the most formidable aircraft ever included in NATO's inventory — and the Harrier's story is by no means ended. Both McDonnell Douglas and British Aerospace are looking well ahead into the 21st Century with further V/STO developments which, for the time being at least, remain locked behind security doors well away from the eyes of the outside world.

Chapter 3
Tornados in action

Towards the end of 1982, a Tornado GR Mk 1 of No IX Squadron, RAF Honington, took off on the longest training flight made by a Tornado up to that date.

On the morning of Monday, 8th November, Flight Lieutenant Ian Dugmore (Pilot) and Squadron Leader Mike Holmes (Navigator) took off from the Suffolk airfield in Tornado *ZA590*, tasked with carrying out a simulated airfield attack against RAF Akrotiri in Cyprus, a return flight of some 4,300 nm — the equivalent of flying from London to Peking.

The purpose of the flight was to prove the concept of a long-range hi-lo-hi sortie, using high and low-level in-flight refuelling. High-level refuelling would be carried out by Victor K 2 tankers, and a Buccaneer of No 237 OCU, also from Honington and carrying a buddy-buddy pod, would be used for low-level refuelling. The Tornado and Buccaneer were to fly together on the outward leg of the sortie.

Soon after take-off, the two aircraft met with the first Victor tanker off the coast of East Anglia to ensure that their refuelling systems were fully serviceable. The outward leg of their route was flown at altitudes varying between 18–24,000 ft and took them over France, Sardinia and Sicily, where they again refuelled from a Victor tanker. The high-level tanker rendezvous was achieved using the Tornado's radar in the air-to-air mode.

After leaving the tanker the two aircraft set course for Cyprus, descending to 2,000 ft 300 miles west of the island for low-level refuelling. The Tornado then left the Buccaneer for the final approach to Cyprus, descending 200 ft and increasing speed to 480 kt at a range of 100 miles in preparation for the simulated airfield attack. As they approached RAF Akrotiri, Squadron Leader Holmes switched on the radar for the final phase of the attack.

He commented: 'It's nice to go such a long distance over the sea and find that when you switch on the radar only a few minutes out from the target, with an offset selected, the offset appears on radar very close to where the computer says it should be. The offset error was so small that for the visual attack we didn't need it — but we would have needed it for an accurate blind attack at night.'

After the successful simulated airfield attack, the Tornado retraced its route back to Sicily for the final high-level refuelling. The return flight at 20–27,000 ft again took them over Sardinia and

A production Tornado F 2 in its pale grey camouflage, carrying four Sky Flash AAMs, two Sidewinder short-range AAMs and two long-range fuel tanks.

France before they finally landed at RAF Honington after being airborne for twelve hours ten minutes.

The flight showed what can be achieved with Tornado, the finest weapons system ever to serve with the Royal Air Force — as well as with the Federal German and Italian air forces, for that matter. Described in a few paragraphs, it all sounds very simple. But let us take a closer look at this remarkable aircraft, and at what goes into a

With wings fully forward, airbrakes extended and flaps down to reduce speed, a Tornado F 2 formates with a Hercules photographic aircraft.

training sortie by a Tornado of one of the RAF's operational squadrons.

The variable-geometry Tornado grew out of a 1960s requirement for a strike and reconnaissance aircraft capable of penetrating the increasing sophistication of the Warsaw Pact air defences by day and night, in all weathers, and of delivering a wide variety of stores with pinpoint accuracy. To achieve this goal it would have to fly at high speed and very low level — less than 150 ft — for most of the distance to the target. The latter, no matter how small or well camouflaged, would have to be located and destroyed in a single pass, for which purpose the aircraft would have to carry the most advanced avionics kit possible. It would, moreover, require plenty of potential for development as a long-range interceptor.

The resulting Multi-Role Combat Aircraft, as the original Tornado concept was known, traced its ancestry to the ill-starred TSR-2 and through the proposed Anglo-French Variable Geometry Aircraft of 1966, both of which were strangled by politics. To develop the new MRCA a consortium of companies was formed under the name of Panavia; it consisted principally of the British Aircraft Corporation (later British Aerospace), Messerschmitt-Bölkow-Blohm and Aeritalia, together with a host of sub-contractors.

The original intention had been to develop a weapons system that would be common to the needs of all three nations, but as time went by this proved impracticable and the three countries involved developed their own modifications to meet their individual needs. Only British Aerospace, for example, pursued the interceptor concept (of which more later), while all three nations produced the weapons fit that was peculiar to their requirements. Nevertheless, the aircraft that emerged was a fine tribute to the international collaboration, and given the divergence of requirements the development phase was not as protracted as it might have been.

The prototype Tornado flew in West Germany on 14 August 1974, followed by the British prototype shortly afterwards at Warton, in Lancashire, and from then on the test and evaluation programme proceeded relatively smoothly despite the loss of Tornado P.08, the weapons trials aircraft, over the Irish Sea on 12 June 1979.

The first Service Tornados were delivered in July 1980 to RAF Cottesmore, and the Tri-National Tornado Training Establishment was formed there in January 1981. The TTTE, which has an establishment of fifty aircraft (21 RAF, 22 Luftwaffe and seven

Italian AF) is responsible for training the Tornado crews of all three nations in the following tasks:

1 Preparing and planning a sortie to include simulated weapons aiming and release.
2 Navigating to, and carrying out low-level simulated attacks on, one or more targets.
3 Carrying out simulated low-level attacks against a mobile 'radar bomb score unit' target.
4 Recognition of electronic warfare threats.
5 Planning and executing escape manoeuvres after an attack.
6 Taking evasive action against an air attack without detracting from the main task.

All Tornados at the TTTE have an operational role in time of war. After conversion at Cottesmore, the aircrews are ready to begin training at their respective national weapons training units; in the RAF's case, the Tornado Weapons Conversion Unit (TWCU) is at Honington and carries the 'shadow' designation of No 45 Squadron. It began operations in January 1982 and has an establishment of 22 aircraft. Its primary task, which is the same as its sister units in Germany and Italy, is to introduce aircrews from the TTTE to the weapons and operational use of the Tornado GR 1, and to develop their navigational techniques. In addition, the TWCU runs a Tornado weapons instructor course, which gives experienced pilots extra flying and ground schooling. Also based at Honington is the Tornado Standards Unit, which ensures that standards and procedures are maintained on the type throughout the RAF and monitors the content of the training courses.

No IX Squadron is based at Honington and was the first operational squadron to receive Tornados. The squadron was officially re-formed on 1 June 1982 and quickly reached its full establishment of thirteen aircraft; deliveries of these, in fact, had begun several months earlier. The squadron reached operational status in the strike/attack role by day and night in the middle of the following year. Meanwhile, No 617 Squadron had also re-formed on the Tornado at Marham early in 1983, to be followed later in the year by No 27 Squadron at the same location. The re-equipment of RAF Germany's Buccaneer and Jaguar squadrons also got under way with the conversion to Tornado of Nos XV, 16 and XX Squadrons at Laarbruch.

The Luftwaffe's Tornado Weapons Conversion Unit was

established in February 1982 with fifteen aircraft and was originally at Erding, 25 miles north-east of Munich, but on 1 July 1983 it moved to Jever, where Waffenschule der Luftwaffe 10 took over the task as Jagdbombergeschwader (JBG) 38. The first operational Luftwaffe Tornado unit was JBG 31 Boelcke at Nörvenich, which exchanged its F-104 Starfighters for the new type in April 1983 and was followed by JBGs 32, 33 and 34. The first German Navy Tornado wing, Marinefliegergeschwader 1, was formed at Jagel (sixty miles south of the Danish border) in July 1982 and was declared operational in the anti-shipping/strike role at the end of the following year. The second Navy Tornado wing, MFG 2, began to hand over its Starfighters in 1986.

In Italy, the first Air Force group to convert to Tornado was 154 Gruppo of 6 Stormo at Ghedi, near Lake Garda. The Gruppo operated F-104s until the middle of 1982. The second Italian Tornado unit is Gruppo 156 (36 Stormo) at Gioia del Colle, Bari, and the third is Gruppo 155, which is also at Ghedi. Tornados also serve with the 3° Gruppo Efficienza Velivoli, a maintenance unit at Cameri, near Milan. As the previous generation of strike aircraft operated by the Italian Air Force were single-seaters, the IAF had no nucleus of navigators/systems operators on which to base their Tornado crews; navigators had to be trained in the United Kingdom and the United States and then fed into the TTTE.

Roll-out of the first two production Tornado ADVs at BAe Warton on 28 March 1984.

Because of its ability to absorb various weapons fits, Tornado has adapted itself very well to the different requirements of the three operator countries (three at the time of writing, that is, in mid-1985). In Italian Air Force service, for example, the Tornado is replacing the F/RF-104G in the air superiority, ground attack and reconnaissance roles, while in Luftwaffe service it is replacing the F-104G in the battlefield interdiction, counter-air and close air support roles. Tornados equipping the German Navy's two wings are tasked with strike missions against sea and coastal targets, and with reconnaissance.

The RAF's Tornado GR Mk 1 is tasked for the interdictor/strike (IDS) role, and when all 220 aircraft are delivered some two-thirds of the Service's front-line aircraft will be Tornados. The type is scheduled to equip seven strike/attack squadrons and one reconnaissance squadron in Germany, where, although the Tornado's function is to deliver a heavy load of conventional stores with great accuracy on targets deep inside enemy territory, it has also been modified to carry tactical nuclear weapons. This leaves one reconnaissance squadron (No 27) and two strike/attack squadrons (Nos IX and 617) based in the UK, together with the Tornados of TTTE and the TWCU.

A typical hi-lo-hi Tornado attack sortie begins in conventional fashion with flight planning, the navigator plotting the route on 1:500,000 charts together with all relevant information such as initial points (IPs), targets, elapsed times, waypoints, diversions and so on. All this data is then transferred from the map to the Cassette Preparation Ground Station (CPGS), an electronic map table, a computer with a keyboard, a VDU and hard copier, and a cassette data recorder. The map is placed on the electronic table and aligned with the computer by placing the cursor over any two grid intersections and then typing in their latitude and longitude, after which the cursor is moved along the route from waypoint to waypoint, entering them in alphabetical order together with the targets.

Once the basic route is entered, then planned groundspeed, fuel load, fuel flow and minimum return fuel are typed in. The printer produces a complete fuel and time plan, and the route co-ordinates are recorded on magnetic tape. The cassette is then taken out to the aircraft to be loaded on to the main computer — a Litef Spirit 3 64K — as the flight plan for that sortie.

With flight planning completed the Tornado crew 'suits up' in standard gear of long underwear, long-sleeve pullover, g-trousers, life-saving jacket (LSJ) (which, unlike the old Mae West, has arms), twin-visor helmet and oxygen mask, gloves, boots and personal equipment connector. Pilot and navigator are then ready to walk to the purpose-built Hardened Aircraft Shelter in which each Tornado is housed, and whose 3 ft thick walls of reinforced concrete are capable of withstanding all but a direct hit by a conventional weapon.

At the aircraft, the pilot starts the Auxiliary Power Unit (APU) after first checking that the right pylons are selected on the weapon programming unit, which is located just forward of the port main undercarriage. The APU, manufactured by KHD in Germany, uses very little fuel and is clutched into the right-hand gearbox, driving the right hydraulic pump and the right alternator to produce about half the normal running hydraulic pressure, although full pressure can be selected for a systems check. The pilot then makes his pre-flight external inspection of the aircraft while the navigator aligns the inertial navigation system, warms up the radar and enters the flight plan.

Strapping into the Martin Baker Mk 10A seats, which provide safe escape at zero altitude and at speeds from zero up to 630 kt, is a

Close-up of the Tornado F 2's cockpit.

simple operation. There is plenty of room for movement in the tandem cockpit. The Tornado crew member sits on his personal survival pack which is clipped to a lanyard on the LSJ; he then fastens his negative g, lap and shoulder straps, leg restrainers below the knees and above the ankles, and arm restraints. The latter are fastened to quick releases on the LSJ, which is the primary reason why the latter has sleeves, and the reason for the extra restrainers is to provide extra safety should the crew have to eject at high airspeeds.

Before starting up the Tornado's twin Turbo-Union RB-199-34R Mk 101 turbofans, each rated at 9,000 lb/st dry and 16,000 lb/st with reheat, let's take a closer look at the aircraft's impressive array of avionics. As one delighted navigator put it: 'Unparalleled authority over the aircraft is given via the "system". When both autopilot and terrain-following radar are engaged, the navigator can supervise a blind low-level mission, including navigation adjustments and updates, weapon selection, arming and automatic release, with very little front-seat assistance. As far as the navigator is concerned, the pilot's main task is to monitor the terrain-following radar and to keep the engines turning.'

The key to the system is the Central Digital Computer, which calculates the aircraft's present position from four sources: the Ferranti FIN 1010 three-axis digital inertial navigation sysem (DINS) which provides primary heading, attitude and velocity; a twin-gyro platform (SAHR) to give secondary heading and attitude; a Decca Type 72 Doppler radar system providing secondary velocity; and a Microtecnica air date computer (ADC) which supplies data such as true airspeed and Mach number.

All this information is exchanged between computer and crew through a variety of channels. In the front cockpit, the pilot's primary source of information is the Smiths/Teldix/OMI electronic head-up display; he also has a GEC Avionics/Aeritalia autopilot and flight director which uses two self-monitoring computers, a GEC/Bodenseewerk triplex command stability augmentation system, a Ferranti projected map display, a GEC terrain-following E-scope display, a Texas Instruments terrain-following radar and a Smiths Industries horizontal situation indicator.

In the rear cockpit, the navigator's avionics equipment includes a TV tabular display produced by GEC in partnership with AEG and Selenia, a combined radar and projected map display, navigation mode panel, Texas Instruments ground mapping radar, stores management system, weapon-aiming mode selector, laser ranger and marked target seeker, passive radar warning receiver and active ECM system.

Using either of the moving maps or TV displays the crew can enter a revised flight plan at any time into the computer, which then — knowing aircraft present position and planned route — can issue steering commands to the HUD, autopilot, horizontal-situation indicator and TV displays. While the pilot monitors the terrain-following radar and therefore the aircraft's low-level flight path, the navigator monitors the progress of the flight on his ground-mapping radar and carries out radar position fixes and weapon aiming; both crew members can update the present position stored in the central computer. Thanks to the stores management system, the navigator can assign weapons to a particular target before flight; when a release signal is received from the main computer, the stores management system automatically drops the correct weapons from their hardpoints.

After aligning the inertial navigation system, the navigator turns his attention to his TV displays. First, one TV is switched to 'Plan' mode, which displays a labelled diagram of the route and checks that the flight plan has been properly entered on the computer; the other two available modes are 'Navigation', which displays all the information necessary to monitor the sortie, and 'Fix/Attack', which is used during position fixing and weapon aiming. The radar/map display presents a projected moving map on one of three scales — 1 mile, $\frac{1}{2}$ mile or $\frac{1}{4}$ mile, with radar information superimposed — and the aircraft's present position is shown as a small circle that moves along the route as the sortie progresses.

Next, the navigator switches on the Doppler radar and twin-gyro platform, selecting 'Navigate' on the INS when alignment is complete. The 'main' mode, in which the computer continuously compares primary and secondary headings and velocities to calculate true values, is the one normally used and is extremely accurate thanks to a process called Kalman filtering, but three other navigation-system modes are available should the Main fail for any reason.

The navigator's next task is to interrogate the stores management system to ensure that the ordnance load is correct, and then allocates the weapons into 'packages' consisting of the type and number of stores to be released at a given time, with appropriate fuze selection. The armourers have already programmed the system with data about what weapons are loaded, and on which pylons. In Tornado, the pilot controls the two fixed 27 mm IWKA-Mauser cannon and air-to-air missiles; the navigator controls all other armament, which depending on operational requirements can consist of the JP233 low altitude airfield attack munitions dispenser, Paveway laser-guided bomb, AS-30, Maverick, GBU-15, Sea Eagle and Kormoran ASMs, napalm, BL-755 Mks 1 and 2 600 lb cluster bombs, MW-1 munitions dispenser, Mk 83 1,000-lb bombs, 'smart' or retarded bombs, BLU-1B 750 lb fire bombs, Matra 500 lb ballistic and retarded bombs, Lepus flare bombs, LAU-51A and LR-25 rocket launchers, active or passive ECM pods, Pave Spike pods, data link pods and chaff/flare dispensers.

Meanwhile, the pilot is occupied with starting-up. The APU is already driving the right gearbox, so pressing the starter switch to 'right' simply clutches in that engine to its own gearbox. The two engine gearboxes can be connected via a cross-drive shaft, and if either engine is lost in the air the cross-drive clutch closes automatically so that no services are lost from the failed engine. The use of this clutch means that either engine can be started first from the APU, and in the air the clutch can be used to crank up a stopped engine at speeds below normal light-up windmill speed.

With the pre-flight checks completed — a procedure made simpler by BITE, Tornado's built-in test equipment, which automatically checks out items such as the command and stability augmentation system and brings them into play — the aircraft is ready to taxi out of the HAS. The navigator punches in the co-ordinates of the HAS into the main computer and the pilot selects idle thrust to move forward. On this sortie the aircraft is carrying stores and is fairly heavy; if it were light, idle thrust would be too high, and in that case the pilot would open the reheat nozzles to a taxi position, reducing the thrust by about thirty per cent.

Outside the HAS, the Tornado halts briefly while the crew remove their ejection seat pins and the pin for the canopy detonating cord, which they show to the ground crew as a safety check before stowing them away. A wave from the crew chief indicates that the aircraft is clear to taxi and it moves forward again, the pilot operating the rudder bar to steer the nosewheel.

In the rear cockpit, the navigator carries out one or two position fixes to instruct the computer on inertial-platform drift. The computer monitors the calculated fix errors, and either an 'A' for accept or 'R' for reject comes up on the right-hand TV display. One

Tornado F 2 being refuelled from a VC-10 tanker of No 101 Squadron.

check involves punching in a preset fix as the aircraft crosses the numbers on the end of the runway in use. The computer is not totally infallible and has been known to come up with an 'R' even though the navigator is certain of his position; in that case he can override it.

The crew makes the final cockpit checks: seat pins out, harness locked and tight, loose articles stowed, oxygen on and functioning normally. The pilot holds the Tornado on the toe brakes, runs up the engines to maximum dry power and then into minimum reheat. Finally, as he releases the brakes, he slams the throttles into maximum reheat. If the aircraft is in overload condition he can engage 'combat' power, an increased temperature rating that can provide extra boost for up to five minutes in every flight.

As the aircraft accelerates along the runway, any tendency to weathercock is compensated to a considerable degree by the nosewheel steering augmentation system, which is gyroscopically controlled. There is little cockpit noise as Tornado gathers speed, and after a twelve-second roll the pilot rotates the nose to a 10° angle of attack, the aircraft leaving the runway cleanly at 150 kt. Gear and flaps come up, and with safe flying speed attained reheat is cancelled. Not only does this reduce noise levels; it also produces low fuel consumption in the cruise with the wing still swept forward.

The flight plan calls for a climb to 25,000 ft over the Wash, then northwards along the coast to the Tyne, followed by a gradual descent and turn-in over the Northumberland coast near Alnwick.

From then on it will be low-level all the way to the first target, a dam wall holding back millions of tons of water in a reservoir north of Dumfries; then south to the second target, a range vessel in Luce Bay, and from there across the Irish Sea to the range off Jurby, in the Isle of Man; then a climb back to 25,000 ft for the transit home to Honington.

For cruise to the target the Tornado is put on to autopilot — track hold, height hold and auto-throttle — and the pilot need not hand-fly the aircraft again until the final landing, as the autopilot pitch channel can be switched from barometric height hold to terrain following when the aircraft is running in towards the target. As the navigator updates the aircraft's position, the autopilot adjusts the track to achieve the correct release solution for an automatic bombing run at, say, 600 kt and 200 ft.

The computer tells the navigator everything he needs to know via the TV display, the aircraft's present position being shown at the centre of a track-orientated display. There is a heading display at the top of the screen, and when the aircraft is on track the heading line is straddled by parallel 'tramlines' at the centre of the screen.

Present aircraft position is also monitored on the radar/map display; the navigator can either correlate the information supplied by the radar and moving map, or check the latter against visual features. If the Tornado is terrain-following, the ground mapping radar can be switched to terrain-avoidance mode — in which it displays all ground terrain above the level of the aircraft — as a safety measure as well as a useful navigational check.

As Tornado climbs to cruising altitude on our sortie the pilot contacts Eastern Radar with en-route details while the navigator sets up his equipment for a fix on the first waypoint; the Humber Estuary and Spurn Head, 80 nm and twelve minutes into the flight with a ground speed of 350 kt.

At any point of the flight the navigator can obtain a fix by making a 'map match', which involves slewing the moving map until it overlays the real world as shown on the radar display. For a planned fix, however, such as this one, he selects Fix/Attack on one TV display. The computer's memory has stored the first waypoint position, so by selecting 'Stabilise' on the radar/map display the navigator instructs the computer to display the waypoint map position and the estimated waypoint radar position, ground-stabilised at the screen centre. The navigator then uses his hand controller to activate a cross in the screen centre; the cross is manoeuvred over the waypoint radar position, once this has been positively identified, and the insert button pressed. The computer calculates the fix update vectors and displays them on the TV screen. After the fix the navigator goes back to monitoring the system; if this were an actual combat sortie in a hostile environment he would be preoccupied with his RWR and ECM systems.

If Tornado has to take avoiding action at high level the pilot accelerates by slamming the throttles to 'Combat' and bringing the wing lever back to the 45° position when the aircraft approaches 0.8M. (0.8M/500 kt is the limiting IAS for the wing swept fully forward in the 25° position.) When fully swept back the wing is at 67°, but 45° gives reduced drag when hard manoeuvring is called for. Tornado's triplex fly-by-wire flight control system gives excellent stability and response at all angles of sweep and with all payloads; full-stick roll rate is identical between zero and four g in

A Tornado F 2 climbs away with reheat engaged.

all three wing sweep positions between 0.5M and 1.0M at all altitudes and with all loads.

If maximum acceleration is required the wing is swept all the way back to 67° at 0.92M, although the 45° sweep angle may be retained until the limiting IAS of 1.6M/600 kt is reached. Apart from a very slight noise increase there is very little indication that the aircraft is coming up to 1.0M, after which the cockpit assumes its usual silence. Tornado is a very quiet aircraft, and cockpit noise is at about the same level as that experienced by the passengers of a cruising widebody jet airliner.

The sortie continues, our Tornado leaving the coast briefly to speed on its track high over the North Yorkshire Moors. We are now 140 nm and twenty minutes into the sortie. We cross the coast again north of Whitby; a few moments later we are abeam the Tees Estuary and the smoke-shrouded complex of Teesside, the home of ICI.

Coming up to 55° North, the latitude of the River Tyne, the pilot calls Border Radar before starting a gradual descent towards the second waypoint and first turning point — Coquet Island, a mile off the Northumbrian coast near Amble. Both crew members lower their visors and check that their harnesses are tight. The Tornado comes down to 250 ft, still over the sea, and the IAS rises to 480 kt. In a moment, the aircraft will enter the designated low-level route that will take it to the target in a series of dog-legs. The route has been very carefully planned to avoid built-up and noise-sensitive areas as far as possible; the crew will treat villages and isolated farms as SAM sites and fly round them.

The Tornado turns in hard over the coast. Border Radar's array of scanners lies over to the right, with Alnwick a few miles further west. Dead ahead lie the Cheviots; the Tornado twists and turns through their valleys, rolling round the flanks of hills and maintaining a steady 250 ft. The air over the Cheviots is turbulent, but the Tornado's ride remains smooth. The wing-mounted spoilers, which provide additional roll control with the wing forward, are switched out of circuit at sweeps greater than 45°, since their effectiveness becomes negligible with high wing angles; the differential tail now provides pitch and roll. Swept fully back, the wing not only attains a lower lift-curve slope, but also reduces its area by about five per cent as the inboard trailing edge tucks into the fuselage — all of which produces unequalled ride comfort in low-level turbulence. The smoothness of the ride at 250 ft and

0.92M, plus the exceptionally low cockpit noise level, add up to a crew environment that is ideal for terrain-following, HUD and track monitoring without distraction or fatigue.

The time to the next waypoint, a few miles north of Kelso, is measured in seconds that reel off on the right-hand TV display. At zero, the Tornado swings left and heads to the north of Galashiels, passing south of Peebles a couple of minutes later to turn hard left again at the junction of the A701 and B712. Talla Reservoir flashes below and the Tornado twists to the east of Moffatt to pick up its IP, another road junction.

Preparation for the attack has already started some miles back, the Tornado taking evasive action to clear imaginary SAM sites. Now, as the IP comes up twelve miles from the target, the navigator selects Fix/Attack, causing the HUD and TV to show attack data, and also selects the relevant pre-planned weapons package. The pilot rolls into his attack run over the IP; at 500 kt the Tornado will cover the last twelve miles in ninety seconds.

The navigator presses 'Stabilise' on the weapons-aiming management system, using offsets to update with a constant stream of fixes, because the target itself will not show up well on radar. Ninety seconds into the run the simulated weapons release is complete, the Tornado streaks across the target and stays low and level as it heads for the hills, still avoiding imaginary SAMs and presenting the smallest possible profile to them. If this had been for real, a spate of water would now be cascading from the reservoir through a shattered dam wall.

Such is the accuracy of Tornado's attack system that it is quite possible to carry out the last radar-marker update four or five miles from the target and for both crew members to be 'hands off' while the Tornado runs through the target area and releases its weapons automatically. The pilot also has a target-of-opportunity selector which enables him to make a visual unplanned attack, while the navigator can make a blind unplanned attack simply by selecting a weapons package and a mode of attack then activating and positioning the radar marker. The aircraft will attack wherever the navigator has placed the marker on the radar/map display.

The Tornado speeds south-west across the hills and valleys of Galloway towards the next objective in Luce Bay, where the crew of the range vessel from Portpatrick have put out a raft carrying a radar reflector. As he approaches the coast west of Glenluce the pilot pulls up a little to avoid the risk of a birdstrike; seagulls and other seabirds are an ever-present danger here, close to the bird sanctuary on the Mull of Galloway.

The pilot flies a racetrack pattern over the Bay and then rolls on to finals, coming back down to 250 ft and accelerating to 520 kt IAS on the run. The practice bomb is released and the Tornado breaks hard left for a second attempt. The range officer calls a good score after each run and then the Tornado is on its way to the final objective off the Isle of Man, keeping well clear of the Mull of Galloway. The thunder of its passage possibly annoys a few intent bird-watchers but the birds themselves take no notice, having long since grown accustomed to this sort of thing.

Still at low level, the Tornado heads out over the Irish Sea. It is now, in the transit phase at 350–400 kt to its target, that the aircraft would be most vulnerable to interception by hostile aircraft, but its evasive manoeuvring capability is first-class. With a flick of the thumb, the pilot can select manoeuvre flap and slat, giving no trim change but converting the aircraft from a high-wing-loading, maximum-range machine into a lower-wing-loading, highly ma-noeuvrable one that can pull maximum rate turns like a dream. Alternatively, the pilot can accelerate to 550 kt IAS and simply pull back the stick; at 550 kt the Tornado goes up like a bullet and is in the tropopause in about ninety seconds.

After completing the second practice bombing run off Jurby the Tornado heads south-east across the Irish sea. As it approaches the Lancashire coast the pilot punches in the afterburners and pulls up into a 35° climb, going back up to 25,000 ft for the high-level transit back to Honington.

Back in the Honington circuit, the pilot flies the aircraft initially with mid-flap and refers to the angle of attack indicator to achieve optimum touchdown speed. With full flap lowered on final approach there is slight buffeting at the flap limiting speed of 200 kt, but this drops away until it is virtually unnoticeable at 135–140 kt. Autopilot and auto-throttle can be used to give an ILS-coupled approach down to 200 ft.

During final approach, the pilot rocks the throttles to the left past a central latch to pre-arm the lift-dump and thrust-reverse system; the system can not be activated accidentally in the air because the aircraft's weight must settle on the undercarriage first. On touchdown, both sets of wing spoilers extend and act as lift dumpers, killing any tendency to bounce, and the reverse-thrust buckets snap closed on whatever approach power is held at the time.

With maximum dry power and full wheel-brakes selected, the Tornado's deceleration is dramatic. As the IAS winds down through 50 kt an audio warning sounds, telling the pilot to throttle back idle reverse to stop the engines reingesting hot gases and also to prevent loose stones from blowing forward towards the intakes. Reverse thrust is cancelled by rocking the throttles back inboard; one engine is then shut down for taxi-ing back to the HAS and the cross-drive clutch closes automatically to keep both hydraulic systems and both generators on line. Tornado's highly effective reverse thrust system brings the aircraft to a stop in about 1,200 ft and makes a braking parachute unnecessary, an important factor when it comes to a quick turnaround.

The Tornado stops in front of the HAS and the engine is kept running. The arrester hook is lowered and the aircraft winched back into the shelter, with engine still running, so that the INS knows where it is on shutdown. The INS error on starting up for the next sortie should therefore be minimal.

During the return flight to Honington, our Tornado passed within a few miles of RAF Coningsby, in Lincolnshire. This is the home of No 229 Operational Conversion unit, which is responsible for training crews to operational standard on the Tornado F 2, the Air Defence Variant of the type.

The Tornado F 2 ADV, which is peculiar to the Royal Air Force, was developed from the basic design to meet an increasing threat to the United Kingdom from a new generation of Soviet bombers. The United Kingdom Air Defence Region covers a huge area stretching

Two production Tornado F 2s of No 229 Operational Conversion Unit, RAF Coningsby.

The prototype Tornado F 2 on the runway at BAe Warton prior to take-off.

from Iceland in the north to the English Channel in the south and also encompasses the sea lanes of the North Atlantic; its defence is of critical importance to NATO.

The Tornado F 2 is a long-range interceptor and is designed to remain on combat air patrol for lengthy periods. Patrol loiter time can be extended to several hours with in-flight refuelling. Its mission is to detect, identify and destroy enemy aircraft approaching the UK ADR at supersonic speeds at high, medium or low altitudes, using its snap-up/snap-down missiles. Its fire-control system is able to engage multiple targets in rapid succession; its weapons systems are highly resistant to enemy ECM; and its good short-field performance enables it to operate, if necessary, from damaged airfields. In carrying out its task the F 2 operates in conjunction with the United Kingdom Air Defence Environment radar system, AEW aircraft and certain radar warning vessels, all linked on a secure and ECM-resistant data and voice command and control net. Such is the F 2's potency that it is able to operate more than 350 nm from its base at night, in bad weather, in heavy ECM conditions, against multiple targets coming in at low level; this means that Tornado F 2s operating from their base at Leuchars, in Scotland, in such conditions, are capable of engaging targets at up to Latitude 64° North, in the so-called Faroes Gap.

Two main airframe changes distinguish the Tornado F 2 from the

IDS variant. The first is an increase in fuselage length of 4 ft 4 in to house the longer radome of the GEC Avionics AI-24 radar and to allow its principal armament of four Sky Flash missiles to be recessed under the fuselage in tandem pairs aft of the rear cockpit. The second is that the fixed inboard portions of the wings are extended forward at the leading edges to give increased chord and compensate for the shift in CG. Two benefits of the fuselage extension are a ten per cent increase in internal fuel capacity and a significant reduction in supersonic drag. Other changes include the deletion of one of the 27 mm Mauser cannon and the installation of uprated RB199 Mk 104 engines. Wing sweep and flap and slat movement is automatic, the wing sweep in response to Mach number, the flap and slat in response to angle of attack.

The Tornado F 2's Foxhunter pulse-Doppler radar uses a

A Tornado F 2 carrying four Sky Flash AAMs two Sidewinder AAMs and two drop tanks poses behind an RAF Hercules for the photographer.

technique known as frequency modulated interrupted continuous wave (FMICW), with which is integrated a Cossor IFF-3500 interrogator and a radar signal processor to suppress ground clutter. The radar's high pulse repetition frequency (PRF) enables it to detect targets at an initial range of about 100 nm, while FMICW allows the range of the target to be determined from the frequency change between transmission and reception.

As they are detected, the targets are stored in the main computer (which is the same as that in the IDS variant). Since the radar continues to scan normally, the targets are unaware that they are the subject of detailed analysis. The system rejects unwanted signals, leaving only real targets which then pass through the radar data processor prior to display to the aircraft's crew. While the radar keeps up a 'running commentary' on ranges, velocities and tracks of established targets, it continues to scan and report new plots.

With the computer fully updated, the crew plan their approach to engage the maximum number of targets. Displays are duplicated in the front cockpit for the pilot, who steers to the engagement on his head-up display. The symbology for Sky Flash, Sidewinder (of

This shot of the Tornado F 2 clearly shows the under-fuselage configuration of the four Sky Flash AAMs.

Tornado F 2 A03 in pale grey camouflage. This was a trials aircraft used to test the Foxhunter AI radar.

which the F 2 can carry four) or gun attacks is very clear, and an important feature is the target indicator which aids the pilot in an early visual sighting.

For a long-range interception, the British Aerospace Dynamics Sky Flash semi-active radar homing AAM would be used. This weapon, which has a high-explosive warhead, has a range of up to thirty miles and is integrated with the aircraft's radar system, being tuned to search in the correct frequency band via its rear reference aerial. The Foxhunter radar illuminates the target scene, and when a hostile is identified within that scene Sky Flash is ready for launch.

As Foxhunter continues to illuminate the target, the reflected radar signals are received by the missile seeker; signals sent by the aircraft are received through the missile's rear reference aerial and are corrected for Doppler shift so that Sky Flash homes on to the correct target. The seeker can separate a close formation of aircraft into individuals and select one for attack; this prevents it from becoming confused and missing the lot, which has been a drawback with earlier generations of AAMs.

The missile launch sequence lasts less than a tenth of a second, the missile being driven down from its fuselage recess by two gas-operated, long-stroke rams developed by Frazer-Nash. These push the missile clear of the airflow and also stabilize it; the rams are retracted immediately after launch to avoid drag.

For interceptions at closer range the AIM-9L Sidewinder would be used. These missiles are carried on the inboard underwing

Above   *Tornado F 2 A01 taking off from Farnborough with two Sky Flash missiles, two Sidewinder AAMs, and two long-range tanks.*

Below   *Tornado F 2 ZA267 launching a Sky Flash AAM during trials.*

stations and, as the Falklands War showed, are excellent in countering a close-in threat. To respond quickly to this kind of threat, the pilot can take control of the radar and weapons systems by selecting the air-to-air override mode. This mode, optimized for visual combat, is controlled by two multi-function buttons mounted on the throttle. Pressing the buttons in sequence selects the close combat radar mode and associated HUD displays, as well as the required weapons, without the pilot having to take his hands off the throttle or the stick. Compared with the long and difficult reach to the armament panel in a Phantom, the system is very easy to use. A hand controller, located aft of the throttles, may be used to slew the radar scanner or missile homing heads if the automatic HUD scan pattern is insufficient to acquire the target. Once the target is in scan, lock-on is automatic.

At low to medium altitudes, the Tornado F 2 is more agile than either the Phantom or the Lightning, the interceptors it was designed to replace and it can also out-accelerate them. In simulated combat between a Tornado F 2 and a Phantom, each aircraft carrying half fuel and external tanks, the Phantom did not once succeed in achieving a realistic position for firing either missiles or guns, both in a head-on pass and when trying to enter a 45° kill cone off the Tornado's tail. The Phantom was out-turned in the horizontal fight, out-manoeuvred in the vertical, out-scissored when slow and could not break off the fight without being caught.

With 67° of sweep and maximum reheat, Tornado F 2 accelerates quickly to 800 kt at low level and 2.0M at high altitude. An indication of its manoeuvrability is that it is quite at home performing full deflection 360° aileron rolls at an indicated airspeed of 750 kt, 1.2M, below 5,000 ft. It is also capable of pulling a 4 g turn at 250 kt and a 6 g turn at slightly over 300 kt, which gives it a turning radius of about 1,500 ft. Nothing except a fighter designed for the limited role of air superiority is going to sit on a Tornado F 2's tail unless the pilot wants it there.

Chapter 4
Hawk: the fighting trainer

At Dunsfold aerodrome, nestling amid the heavily-wooded Surrey countryside a few miles south-east of Godalming, it looks like being a routine day. It is here that British Aerospace test their Hawks and Harriers prior to delivery, and this morning a 60-Series Hawk is about to be put through its paces by a BAe Test Pilot, accompanied by a Flight Test Engineer, prior to a delivery flight that will take it to Zimbabwe.

The Hawk has a rather odd appearance, for it is finished only in yellow/green primer. The final paintwork will be completed as the last item before the aircraft is handed over to the customer.

Particular attention is paid on a production test flight to the correct functioning of every item in the aircraft, even down to measuring and recording the force needed to operate each control. It takes a good deal of time and is painstaking work, so that it may be nearly an hour from the time of the crew walking out to the aircraft before they are ready for engine start.

Start-up clearance is obtained from Air Traffic Control and the main test begins. Fuel pump on, anti-collision beacon on, and the start button is pressed. The Hawk's gas turbine starter begins to accelerate; fifteen seconds later an indicator on the panel shows green and the main engine start sequence commences. High pressure air is fed to the starter turbine and the Hawk's Adour engine starts to rotate. As the RPM increase, the pilot opens the throttle to the idle position and the high energy igniters initiate combustion.

A deep rumble indicates engine light-up, and a few moments later the start sequence shuts down automatically as the Adour reaches its idle speed. Electrics and hydraulics come on line and fuel flow stabilises at around 350 lb/hr. Navigation and communication systems are switched on after start checks are run, and the aircraft is ready to move. Air Traffic gives clearance to the runway, and on the way the brakes and steering are tested and the pre-take-off checklist completed. Canopy fully locked, ejector seats live, harness secure, all systems functioning, and the crew run through their take-off emergency briefing.

The final items are completed when the Hawk is lined up for take-off. The engine is run up to full power and the pilot checks engine response, temperature and open limiting and fuel flow. Air Traffic gives departure clearance for runway 25, with instructions to maintain runway heading up to 2,000 ft, followed by a right turn heading 280° and a call to Farnborough Control.

With fuel flow showing 4,000 lb/hr and the engine temperature at its limit of 640° the brakes are released. Acceleration is rapid and the aircraft reaches its take-off speed of 125 kt in fifteen seconds. The pilot rotates the nose for lift-off and the aircraft climbs steeply at around 30° in a noise abatement departure, reaching an altitude of 2,000 ft by the time it is over the end of Dunsfold's 7,000 ft runway.

After contact with Farnborough Control more checks are completed. The operation of the landing gear is checked at low speed, and then the speed is increased to 450 kt to check control functions, trim settings and angle of attack.

Farnborough gives climb clearance now to 45,000 ft. The climb is flown initially at 350 kt, converting at higher altitude to 0.72M.

The Hawk has enjoyed considerable export success: this example is a Hawk Mk 52 for the Air Force of Zimbabwe and carries 130-gallon drop tanks for long-range ferry.

Engine and aircraft performance are recorded throughout and the aircraft passes 30,000 ft some five minutes after take-off. During the climb, control passes from Farnborough to London Military Radar which provides an outstanding level of assistance to the busy crew, flying as they are in the very crowded airspace of Southern England. The aircraft's IFF system provides the radar control not only with an enhanced blip on the radar display, but also with an identification and a readout of altitude.

As the climb takes the Hawk over the gliding centre at Lasham the crew can see the Solent away to the left, with the Isle of Wight standing out clearly and the Bristol Channel ahead. At around 30,000 ft London Control requests a left turn heading 150° for the Hawk to position south of St Catherine's point on the southern tip of the Isle of Wight. The first test after the climb is a supersonic run, which must be carried out over the sea.

As the aircraft crosses the Solent the altitude reaches 40,000 ft, still less than ten minutes from take-off. The rate of climb has now reduced to around 2,000 ft/min, fuel flow in the thin cold air is down to about 1,200 lb/hr and the cabin has become very quiet. The crew can clearly hear the sound of their own breathing in the intercom system.

London gives permission for the supersonic dive. The aircraft is rolled inverted and the nose drops to a 60° dive angle. The speed increases very rapidly. At 0.88M there is a transient shuddering, at 0.92 a brief disturbance in roll, and then the machine is supersonic — no buffeting or vibration is evident and the speed typically reaches about 1.1M. The limit is 1.2M.

At supersonic speeds the aircraft remains responsive and it is easy to forget that height is being lost at over 1,000 ft per second. Dive recovery starts at 30,000 ft, initially at 2.5–3 g. The crew's g suits inflate, squeezing abdomen and legs to prevent blood pooling in the lower body and help avoid 'grey out'.

As the speed becomes subsonic the g increases to about +5, and seconds later the Hawk is out of the dive and climbing again. The next item on the list is a check of the cabin pressure warning. At 35,000 ft the cabin air pressure is to be switched off, and as a vital preliminary the crew check their oxygen and tighten their face masks. As the system is turned off the pressure in the cabin falls dramatically. The cockpit fills with mist and in seconds a loud hooter and a red warning light on the central warning panel confirm the loss of pressure. It is an uncomfortable experience for the crew, and almost as uncomfortable as the pressure is selected on again. In the space of about five seconds, they have effectively been to the top of Mount Everest and back.

Further checks follow. An engine 'slam' (a test of maximum acceleration) at 30,000 ft — an airborne light-up of the gas turbine starter to confirm its operation in its secondary role as a back-up system for restarting the engine in flight — a trim check at maximum level speed at 15,000 ft — and it is time for the stall tests.

These are done at 10,000 ft and control is handed over to Boscombe Down, the Aircraft and Armament Experimental Establishment in Wiltshire. Permission is received to commence the tests with a minimum altitude of 8,000 ft, because Boscombe is operating numerous aircraft in the area at lower levels.

The first stall is in the clean or cruise configuration — gear and flaps retracted, airbrake in. The fuel state is recorded so that the exact weight of the aircraft is known, power set to 70 per cent, and

Artist's impression of a T-45A Hawk in the livery of the United States Navy. The T-45A is being modified by British Aerospace and McDonnell Douglas to make it capable of operating from aircraft carriers: 300 aircraft are planned.

the slow deceleration commences. The nose rises almost imperceptibly as the speed reduces with the angle of attack progressively increasing. There is a faint burbling at 9° AoA as the airflow over the wing starts to separate. At 10–11° the buffeting becomes quite pronounced, although control still remains adequate. Finally, at 14–15°, the nose drops and the Hawk wallows in roll, fully stalled.

Next the stall is checked in the landing configuration, with gear down and 50° of flap set. Power is set to 85 per cent to simulate the power setting on a landing approach. The behaviour remains much the same as before but the speeds are lower, the stall occurring at about 95 kt. More systems tests follow — emergency air driven hydraulic pump, fuel and oil pressure warnings — and the aircraft is then taken up to 30,000 ft for spinning.

London resumes control and directs the pilot to a clear area, requesting a call on entering and completing each spin. Pre-spinning checks are carried out — straps tight, flaps and airbrake retracted, hydraulics normal, throttle idle. At 160 kt the pilot applies full rudder and full back stick. The Hawk shudders and rolls with the nose dropping rapidly. The rudder pedals shake violently and a lot of force is needed to hold full control. Most of the instruments are impossible to follow as they fluctuate and gyrate but the altimeter faithfully shows the rapid loss of altitude. The motion is apparently lazy but the aircraft is losing several hundred feet every second.

Recovery from the spin is almost immediate as soon as the controls are centralised. The rotation stops in two to three seconds and the pull-out from the resultant near-vertical dive is complete by 20,000 ft.

After two or three spins, the pilot takes the Hawk down to low altitude for what is physically the most demanding part of the mission, and one that always astonishes pilots not familiar with the aircraft. This is the maximum speed check, followed by a turn at the maximum allowable g.

First the aircraft is accelerated to 575 kt as it passes through 2,000 ft in a shallow dive, then the height is held at 2,000 ft until the speed stabilizes at its maximum level value. This varies a little with temperature, but is around 560 kt. Fuel flow steadies at about 4,500 lb/hr and checks confirm that the engine limiters are operating correctly. Speed is then reduced to 500 kt and the maximum g turn is entered.

At a crushing +8 g the rate of turn is very high and the crew find difficulty in holding up their heads. Despite the g suits, they will find their period of useful consciousness at this g level quite short — around thirty seconds. Astonishingly the aircraft's speed decays only very slowly. After a complete 360° turn at +8 g, the speed is still around 450 kt.

Only a few tests remain before recovery to base — some avionics checks, confirmation of the fuel low warning, and the Hawk returns to Dunsfold. In the circuit, speed is reduced to below 200 kt and the flaps and gear are lowered. The added drag is countered by the power being increased to 85 per cent. Speed is reduced until the angle of attack shows the right value — 5.5° — and the landing approach is commenced.

Clearance to land is given and the Hawk crosses the runway threshold at a little over 100 kt, descending at about 10 ft per second. A gentle flare reduces the rate of sink, the main wheels touch, and the brake parachute is streamed. It deploys with a tremendous tug and with full brake the Hawk stops in a very short distance.

The total flight has taken 1 hour 25 minutes. Any minor adjustments necessary will be noted by the pilot on the Flight Adjustment Form and the aircraft will be prepared for its second flight, which normally involves carrying external tanks to check fuel transfer.

This account gives an idea of what it is like to fly the Hawk — one of the most superlative little military aircraft ever to be developed by the British aircraft industry, and one which, as well as serving the Royal Air Force in considerable numbers, has secured orders from several foreign air forces in the face of stiff competition.

Although it started life strictly as a multipurpose jet trainer for the RAF, the Hawk has since been developed into an outstanding combat aircraft in its own right. A heavy ordnance capability of up to 6,800 lb, a basic design which has required little modification since the type's inception and flying characteristics that endear it to all pilots have combined to place Hawk in a category of its own.

The Hawk's excellent handling qualities have made it an ideal mount for the Red Arrows aerobatic team, through whose display flying it has become well known to the public. New pilots for the Red Arrows undergo the Hawk conversion or refresher course at RAF Valley on Anglesey, which is the home of No 4 Flying Training

The Cessna A-37 is a good example of a light attack aircraft that was developed from a two-seat trainer in the 1960s. Compare its rather cluttered cockpit layout with that of the British Aerospace Hawk T 1 on the right.

School; the first Hawks were delivered there in November 1976 and the school is responsible for the advanced training of pilots destined for fast jets. They undergo a 22-week course at Valley, involving 75 hours' flying, before moving on to a Tactical Weapons Unit. For experienced pilots coming to the Red Arrows, with between 1,500 and 2,000 hours and two tours on fast jets to their credit, the Hawk course is refreshingly simple, consisting of two days of ground school, learning the systems, and two days of simulator plus flying, learning the emergency procedures and getting the feel of the aircraft. Those who have flown the Hunter say that the Hawk is similar but better in all respects, especially range; the Hawk will go further clean than a Hunter with a full load of drop tanks. The aircraft's outstanding handling qualities make it possible to pull 7 g in a Hawk until it runs out of fuel. The aircraft is completely free of vices, unlike some of its contemporaries, which suffer from aileron reversal at high Mach numbers, unpredictable spin modes and buffeting at only mild g levels in turns.

Student pilots who successfully complete their 22-week course at

How the public sees the Hawk: three aircraft of the Red Arrows, the Royal Air Force aerobatic team, taking off from a mist-shrouded Kemble aerodrome.

Valley then move on to a Tactical Weapons Unit, either No 1 at Brawdy in South Wales or No 2 at Chivenor, in Devon. Here the student again flies the Hawk but in a completely different environment and syllabus in which he will learn to use the aircraft as a weapons system. Even the aircraft themselves are representative of their respective roles — red, white and light grey for Valley's trainers, and camouflage at the TWU. The latter's aircraft are usually equipped with the 30 mm Aden cannon on the centreline weapon station and may have practice bomb carriers on the wing pylons.

Both TWUs are organised into so-called 'shadow' squadrons, all of which have a wartime role. The squadrons at Brawdy are Nos 79, 63 and 264; the last two are responsible for taking students from advanced training at Valley to OCU entry and for teaching them the basics of low-level tactical flying, air combat and weaponry, the whole course lasting four months, while No 79 Squadron runs a two-month short course for pilots returning to fast jets after a break from operational flying. At Chivenor, the two squadrons are Nos 63 and 151.

Broadly, the function of the two TWUs is to teach pilots to fight, not to fly. The course is progressively demanding, being designed to filter out all those who are not able to attain, and more importantly maintain, the capacity to cope with the very high workload required in today's front-line tactical squadrons. Those who fail to attain the high standards of the TWU are re-channelled to the support, transport or helicopter roles.

A formation of Hawks from RAF Chivenor, No 2 Tactical Weapons Unit, breaking to join the circuit. All aircraft bear the markings of No 151 'shadow' Squadron, and the code letters on their fins spell out the name of their home airfield.

Flying activity at both TWUs is intense. The average daily sortie rate is about 85, but on occasions — when bad weather has interfered with the training programme, for example — this can be stepped up to 120 a day or even more. Turnround with the Hawk is rapid, thanks to the simplicity of the aircraft's design, and ranges from thirty minutes for an unarmed aircraft to an hour or so if an armed sortie is required.

There is very little dual flying at either TWU. Generally, dual sorties are flown only when it is necessary to initiate a student into a new phase of the training programme, or for type conversion when an experienced pilot passes through the TWU on the refresher course, or to give student navigators experience of high-g back-seat flying before they go on to an OCU. In the normal course of events the Hawks fly two-ship sorties, the student flying solo in one aircraft with his instructor keeping him company in another. TWU instructors work hard, flying up to three one-and-a-quarter hour sorties, each one preceded by a 45-minute briefing and followed by an hour-long debrief.

A student arrives at the TWU from Valley with a pair of brand-new wings on his chest and about 100 hours on the Hawk to his credit, and his TWU initiation usually begins with two rides in the Hawk simulator, during which he flies two complete sorties with emergencies thrown in. By the time the two sorties have been completed the student's flying ability has been assessed pretty

Two Hawk T 1s of No 4 FTS, RAF Valley. XX235 bears the pyramid and palm tree insignia of No 4 FTS, recalling the school's distinguished service in Iraq.

thoroughly and he is ready for his first familiarization flights in the real aircraft. The general handling phase usually starts at high level, working progressively down to 250 ft as the student's confidence increases. The next phase involves tactical formation flying with two and four aircraft; a four-ship formation consists of two elements 1,000 to 1,500 yd apart, each element made up of a leader and a wingman flying up to 200 yd apart.

Air combat training begins with what is known as the 'cine' phase. After a thorough grounding in the mechanics and use of gunsights the student flies a number of sorties with his instructor and tries to keep the latter's manoeuvring aircraft in his sight; his efforts are recorded on film and this is analysed on the ground. Following these essential preliminaries the student is ready for actual air combat experience, starting with the basic one-versus-one and moving up to four-versus-one as experience is gained. Early air combat engagements are flown at high altitude, but once the student has shown a thorough knowledge of the necessary basic skills, engagements move to low level; a typical air combat sortie towards the end of this phase might start with a 'bounce' on a student flying at 250 ft, followed by a climbing fight up to about 10,000.

Students practice air-to-air gunnery against a banner towed by a Hunter, the aircraft's cannon firing inert ball ammunition painted to leave a scoring mark on the target. A record of the student's score is kept throughout this phase to introduce an element of competition and generally encourage overall improvement. This phase is followed by low-level training, which encompasses tactical formation flying, navigation, air-to-ground weapons, rocketing, bombing and strafing. TWU students quickly become familiar with the Pembrey weapons range near Llanelli, where they practice ground attack using cannon, practice bombs and inert 2.75-in rockets. After students have gained experience in the use of each individual weapon they fly composite ground-attack sorties, using all three.

All the training so far has been building up to what most students regard as the high spot of the four-month course: the Simulated Attack Profile (SAP). It is certainly the most demanding. Bringing all his newly-acquired skills into play, each student must fly a series of simulated attacks on designated targets, and in the later stages he is given the chance to plan the entire sortie himself. This phase of training begins with a thorough briefing and a dual sortie with an instructor, followed by two-ship and four-ship sorties which are led by selected students. Planning for SAPs can last five or six hours,

Symbolic of the Hawk's versatility, this aircraft of No 1 TWU, RAF Brawdy, carries two Sidewinder AAMs and a Sea Eagle anti-ship missile as it turns in towards a County-class guided missile destroyer.

because there is much to be considered — not least the avoidance of noise-sensitive areas. The sorties combine tactical formation flying, low-level navigation and a cine attack with weapons delivery, and towards the end of this phase an air combat ingredient is introduced by aggressor aircraft waiting to bounce the attackers en route and in the vicinity of the target.

TWU Hawks, with their high sortie rate, are hard-worked aircraft, and keeping them fit requires a lot of backup on the ground. The same goes for all military aircraft, of course, but for the man in the street, fast-jet flying means the man (or men) in the cockpit; the role of the men on the ground tends to be eclipsed. But flying and fighting modern jets is a team effort demanding 100 per cent dedication from all concerned; if any cog in the wheel ceases to function so does the wheel, possibly with disastrous consequences. So let's take a look at what happens to a TWU Hawk between sorties, and make a mental note not to forget the 'plumbers'. The procedure is more or less the same for all military jets, with minor variations.

Once returning aircraft have landed and are taxi-ing back towards their respective flight lines, it is the task of a junior tradesman to marshal the Hawks to their parking slots. Once the aircraft has rolled to a stop it is the tradesman's job to make safe any remaining ordnance by re-installing the weapon and pylon safety pins. In the same phase, he checks the tyres for abnormal wear, cuts or other damage and then signals the pilot to roll the aircraft forward again — about half a wheel revolution to check the hidden parts of the tyre tread as well as the tyre walls and the wheel itself. The aircraft is now in its final parked position and restraining chocks are emplaced.

Once the pilot has shut down the engine and replaced the safety pins in the Martin Baker Mk 10 ejection seat and miniature detonating cord system he vacates the aircraft, leaving it to the 1st Line man to fit the engine intake blanks. These prevent accidental entry into the duct of any foreign object which could result in FOD — Foreign Object Damage. Having made the aircraft safe against FOD, the tradesman is now able to deal with the turnround itself.

The first stage of the turnround is to refuel, an operation carried out regardless of whether the aircraft is to fly again or be returned to the hangar. It is much safer to have an aircraft fully fuelled than to have it half full of combustible fumes. Refuelling is an extremely rapid operation as the bowsers react quickly to the needs of returning aircraft and are often standing by during the first preliminary safety checks. While these are being done, the bowser driver removes the fuel hose and assists in the preparation for fuel transfer. The actual transfer takes less than five minutes, and when completed the aircraft and bowser gauges are checked for compatible readings.

Having refuelled the aircraft, the line engineer turns his attention to checking the various indicators for fuel, oil and hydraulic accumulator levels as well as the hydraulic systems. He also records the fatigue index reading from the fatigue meter housed in the aircraft's forward avionics bay and logs this on the Form 700, from which the Flight Servicing Certificate is compiled. He will also complete other visual checks and a cockpit inspection for foreign objects/loose articles before indicating that the aircraft is now ready for rearming or a role change, depending on requirements.

Rearming is carried out by a two-man team of qualified RAF armourers, who are responsible for reloading the centreline 30 mm Aden gun or replenishing the practice bomb carriers emptied during the previous sortie. Should the sortie have involved air-to-air combat training, or weapon delivery training, any film taken will also be removed by an avionics technician and replaced, if so required. The film will be processed for student debriefing.

Providing no malfunction has been discovered, the aircraft is now

Hawk T 1 of No 1 TWU landing at RAF Brawdy. Note the practice bomb dispenser under the outboard wing pylon.

ready for its next sortie. If a fault is found by a tradesman on the Line, it is reported to the Rectification Team who in turn allocate the appropriate tradesman to deal with the task. Most of the snags discovered at this stage can usually be rectified without moving the aircraft back into the hangar and are completed within the normal turnround time of one hour. Should the pilot discover a fault during his sortie and report it, the appropriate tradesman will again be called, but in this case it is the responsibility of the technician to debrief the pilot and determine as precisely as possible the source and cause of the fault.

Typical faults at this stage might require a wheel change (in the event of tyres damaged on landing), replacing fuses, flight recorder and electrical units; all of which are classed as Cat One — routine repair/replacement. Should the repair be too complicated or time-consuming to be dealt with on the Line, the aircraft would be removed to the hangar, where it would be rectified either by the 1st Line/2nd Line teams or the defective part would be removed for rectification in one of the Engineering Wing's specialist bays.

For scheduled servicings, the Hawk goes through five separate phases before the cycle begins again. Its first routine service, which occurs every 125 flying hours, is designated the Primary and is completed by the squadron engineering flights in about one day, subject to special instructions or embodiments of important modifications. Items checked, changed or repaired during the Primary can involve wheels, undercarriage, tailplane and canopy, together with work to rectify snags. The latter tasks can take as little as one hour, or as long as two or three days; it is the nature of the job itself and the manpower availability that dictates whether it will be done by the 1st Line, not simply the estimated time for the task.

The 'Primary Star' Servicing follows at every 250 flying hours and is handled by the 2nd Line. In this case the aircraft can be expected to be out of the Line for about nine working days, during which a more in-depth examination takes place. Primary Star servicing, however, also includes the checks required in the Primary — a system that is common to all RAF aircraft servicing procedures.

The 2nd Line crews also deal with the 'Minor' servicing which occurs every 500 flying hours and which requires about twenty working days. This is also the time required for 'Minor Star', every 1,000 flying hours; a 'Major', which is carried out at the 2,000-hour mark, needs sixty working days.

Running parallel to these scheduled servicings are tasks involving the embodiment of larger modifications; these are carried out either at RAF Abingdon, where the Aircraft Servicing Wing is responsible for major overhauls of both Hawk and Jaguar, or by British Aerospace at Dunsfold. One of the more important modifications carried out at Dunsfold involved the conversion of ninety Hawk T 1s to carry two AIM-9L Sidewinder missiles for use in the emergency wartime role of point-defence interception. The Mk 1A

These two photographs show to good advantage the Hawk's armament of two Sidewinder AAMs, carried on the outer wing pylons in the short-range air defence role, and the 30 mm Aden centreline gun pod.

Sidewinder Mod, as it is known, required up to 65 working days per aircraft.

At the time of writing, in 1985, Hawks serve with the air forces of Finland, Indonesia, Kenya, Kuwait, the United Arab Emirates and Zimbabwe as well as with the Royal Air Force. In addition, 300 aircraft are to be built jointly by British Aerospace and the McDonnell Douglas Corporation as the T-45A, for service with the United States Navy from 1991.

In the strike role, Hawk can carry 7,000 lb of stores on six underwing stations. Armament options include air-to-air missiles such as Sidewinder and Magic, air-to-surface weapons like Sea Eagle, and even torpedoes of the Sting Ray type. A Series 100 Enhanced Ground Attack Hawk is under development, featuring a hands-on-throttle-and-stick weapon system comprising inertial nav/attack, headup display/weapon-aiming computer, colour head-down display, stores management system, radar altimeter, radar warning receiver and chaff/flare dispenser, all linked by a 1553B digital databus. A laser rangefinder is an optional extra.

Nor does the story end there. In 1984 British Aerospace announced the launching of the single-seat Hawk 200, the first new fighter programme in the United Kingdom for over a decade. The decision to develop the new aircraft was taken as a result of the rapid growth in costs associated with today's front line aircraft and their growing complexity. A small subsonic aircraft with sophisticated avionics and heavy payload capability can effectively perform the same roles — but being less expensive it can be acquired and deployed in greater numbers, resulting in an increased target coverage.

Past attempts to produce cost-effective small fighting aircraft have generally failed because, although inexpensive, they were unable to carry adequate loads over appropriate distances. Also they were too small to carry the sensors needed for night and all-weather operations. The single-seat Hawk represents a clear breakthrough in these fields and offers unique operational cost-effectiveness. Advanced aerodynamics and design layout permit a disposable load of fuel and ordnance approaching 150 per cent of airframe weight. The highly economical Adour engine makes efficient use of fuel, leading to very long range (over 2,500 miles) and endurance (more than five hours).

The Hawk 200 retains a high degree of commonality with its predecessors, all the changes having been confined to the nose and

The Hawk 200 is a bold attempt by British Aerospace to capture a wide market for a low-cost, high performance strike fighter combining the advantages of light weight with a heavy offensive payload and advanced avionics. Although a dramatic new development, the Hawk 200 retains a high degree of airframe commonality with its predecessors.

The cockpit of the Hawk 200 represents the latest state of the art equipment: pilot workload is eased with the introduction of advanced avionics including HUD, INAS, HOTAS, Digital Databus and colour multi-purpose electronic display.

cockpit fuselage section. The removal of the second seat enables the aircraft to feature two built-in high-velocity 25 mm Aden guns, each with 100 rounds, replacing the current single 30 mm Aden gun pod; this in turn releases the fuselage weapon station for additional ordnance, fuel or an ECM pod.

The Hawk 200 provides operators with a choice of three forward fuselage equipment options to cover the full operational spectrum required by any air arm in any location throughout the world, whether for defence or strike, over land or sea, by day or night and in virtually any weather conditions. For daytime operation the equipment package consists of a gyro-stabilized attack sight together with attitude and heading reference system, or inertial navigation system with headup display, plus weapon aiming computer, digital databus and optional laser ranging. For night operation the aircraft is fitted with forward-looking infra-red (FLIR), converting low light conditions to daytime standards and enabling accurate ground attack and tactical reconnaissance missions to be flown 24 hours a day, while for all-weather operation the package includes advanced multi-mode radar for target acquisition and navigation.

As with its predecessors, Hawk 200's excellent handling and flying qualities remain unimpaired even when carrying large, heavy warloads. It can carry an exceptionally wide range of ordnance, including 2.7-in (68 mm) rockets, runway denial and tactical strike bombs, retarded and cluster bombs, air-to-air and air-to-surface missiles and a variety of external fuel tanks.

In the Airspace Denial role, Hawk 200 is designed to loiter at 30,000 ft with two Sidewinder-type missiles (Sky Flash, AMRAAM, ASRAAM etc) and two external 860 litre fuel tanks. The aircraft can remain on station for four hours at 100 nm from base, two hours at 425 nm, and one hour at 600 nm. Maximum intercept radius is 770 nm. In the Close Air Support role, lo-lo radius is 135 nm with a 6,000 lb warload; in the Interdiction role hi-lo-hi radius is 540 nm with a 5,000 lb warload; and in the Reconnaissance role the total range is 1,950 nm. Armed with two Sea Eagle ASMs in the anti-shipping role, Hawk 200 has a hi-hi radius of 800 nm, equipped with two 860 litre fuel tanks, and the same tankage gives the aircraft a range of 2,200 nm for ferrying or long-range deployment.

Hawk 200 possesses the clean, symmetrical lines that have characterized the best British combat aircraft designs, and its potency is undeniable. Moreover, its small profile would greatly enhance its survivability in action, even against heavily-defended targets; this was proven over Vietnam — the most heavily-defended area of airspace in history — by the McDonnell Douglas A-4 Skyhawk, a larger and heavier aircraft than the Hawk.

Over the years, the A-4 has admirably fulfilled the requirements of many air forces operating on strictly limited budgets, but development of the American design has been pushed just about as far as it will go. On the other hand, the development story of the Hawk, Britain's fighting trainer, is still in its early days.

Chapter 5
The F-14: Grumman's big cat

On 21 December 1970, the prototype Grumman F-14 Tomcat took off on its maiden flight from Long Island. Developed in response to a growing threat from a new generation of Soviet combat aircraft — in particular the Tu-26 Backfire, whose long range and formidable array of air-to-surface weaponry posed a serious menace to US naval task forces — the Tomcat is still, fifteen years later, the most potent interceptor in service anywhere in the world.

Grumman's big naval fighter leaped briefly into the world's headlines on 19 August 1981, when two aircraft of Fighting Squadron VF-41, piloted by Commander Henry Kleeman and Lieutenant Lawrence Muczynski destroyed two Libyan Air Force Su-20 Fitters over the Mediterranean.

The Tomcats were launched from the aircraft carrier USS *Nimitz* at 04:05 GMT to patrol an area 60 nm north of the Libyan coast over the Gulf of Sirte. Fifteen vessels of the United States Sixth Fleet, including the carriers *Nimitz* and *Forrestal*, were conducting a missile firing exercise in the southern Mediterranean at the time. Although the exercise area was clearly defined and the standard international warning issued several days earlier, no fewer than 35 patrols of Libyan aircraft had approached the zone and six aircraft had actually infringed it. In all cases, the Libyans had been intercepted and turned back by Sixth Fleet fighters.

On this occasion, the Tomcat patrol flown by Kleeman and Muczynski was one of several tasked with protecting the perimeter of the exercise area against potentially hostile incursions. At 05:20 GMT, while orbiting at 20,000 ft, Kleeman's weapons officer picked up a radar contact some 40 nm to the south and heading in their direction. The fighter controller directed both Tomcats to investigate and they turned south, with Kleeman in the lead and Muczynski a mile and a half to the rear and slightly higher.

The two radar returns continued to close head-on with the Tomcats, and shortly the weapons officers of both American aircraft reported that their equipment had locked on to transmissions from Soviet-made SRD-5M 'High Fix' air interception and fire control radars operating in the I-Band. This type of radar was known to be contained in the Fitter's intake centrebody, and provided the Americans with the first indication of the type of aircraft they were about to encounter.

Just before the Fitters came in visual range, at about eight miles, the Tomcats started a hard counter-break to starboard towards the contacts to cancel out the Libyans' already marginal missile launch window. The Fitters were visual at between six and seven miles and the Americans saw that they were flying in close formation, with wingtips about 500 ft apart, at about two o'clock on a reciprical heading. The Tomcat pilots turned again to keep the Fitters in sight and rendezvous with them, and as Kleeman passed 500 ft above and about 1,000 ft in front he saw one of the Fitters launch an AA-2 Atoll infra-red homing missile from its starboard pylon. He told Muczynski that they were being fired on and continued a very hard left turn across the Fitters' tails, keeping them in sight all the while and causing the Atoll to break lock as its seeker reached its gimbal limits.

Both Tomcats had broken hard left, and now Kleeman saw the lead Fitter — the one that had fired the Atoll — enter a climbing left-hand turn towards Muczynski and pass through the loop of the American's maximum-rate turn, still climbing. As his wingman rolled out of the turn and went after the lead Fitter, Kleeman reversed his own turn, rolling out to the right in pursuit of the Libyan wingman. He waited ten seconds until his target had crossed the sun, then fired an AIM-9L Sidewinder from a range of about 1,300 yd. The missile struck the Fitter in the tailpipe area, causing the Libyan pilot to lose control, and he ejected within five seconds. Muczynski, meanwhile, had also fired a Sidewinder from about 800 yd, and this too destroyed its target. The pilot of the second Fitter was not seen to eject. The time from the first radar contact to the kills was under sixty seconds.

The two Fitters had been destroyed by a combination of superior tactics, superior weapons and vastly superior aircraft. From the moment they had first been detected by the Tomcats' radar, the Libyans had stood little chance of inflicting damage on their opponents.

The Grumman F-14 Tomcat provided the US Navy with the most advanced weapons system in the world. The aircraft depicted belongs to VF-142, USS Dwight D. Eisenhower.

The F-14 Tomcat forms the interceptor element of a USN Carrier Air Wing, which consists of 90–95 aircraft in the case of a 95,000-ton nuclear-powered vessel of the *Nimitz* class; two squadrons of F-14s are deployed aboard each attack carrier. The big carriers themselves form the nucleus of a US fleet's Battle Force, which is the principal task force; TF-60, in the case of the Mediterranean-based Sixth Fleet. The Fleet has seven more task forces, ranging from TF-61, which is responsible for amphibious landings, to TF-69, which comprises attack submarines.

In the carrier's busy launch cycle the Tomcats are usually away first, providing CAP over the remainder of the launch programme. Launch cycles are planned around a basic period of 1 hour 45 minutes, which is the average time between launch and recovery for the shorter-endurance types. The first wave to launch will recover and land just after the second wave launches, and so on. Longer-endurance aircraft such as the S-3 and E-2 fly a double cycle of three and a half hours. Aircraft to be flown are 'spotted' by the deck control officer in order of launch, with a couple of spare slots aft to accommodate aircraft that may become unserviceable after moving from their own slot.

Let's join a Tomcat crew briefed to fly a CAP mission, and see what it involves. First, a tour around the aircraft itself.

The F-14A Tomcat is described as a two-seat carrier-based multi-role fighter, which in no sense indicates the powerful beast that it really is. It has a variable-geometry wing that can be swept from 20° in the fully forward position to 68°; the sweep angle is programmed automatically throughout the flight envelope, but the pilot can override this manually if necessary. Power for the beast is provided by a pair of Pratt & Whitney TF30-P-414A turbofans producing 20,900 lb/st; the Navy wanted more powerful engines, but even as it is the 414s give the Tomcat a take-off roll with afterburner, at typical combat weight, of only 1,100 ft. They will also push the aircraft to a maximum low-level speed of 792 kt (1.2M) and a high-altitude speed of 1,342 kt, or 2.34M.

The Tomcat's pilot and weapons officer sit in tandem on Martin Baker GRU7A rocket-assisted zero-zero ejection seats under a one-piece bubble canopy that hinges at the rear and gives an excellent all-round view. They have at their disposal the formidable Hughes AN/AWG-9 weapons control system, which is able to detect airborne targets at ranges of up to 170 nm, depending on their size; small targets such as cruise missiles can be detected at 65 nm. The system can track 24 targets and attack six of them at the same time, at a variety of altitudes and ranges. The aircraft is fitted with a Kaiser Aerospace AN/AVG-12 vertical and head-up display system, and an infra-red seeker/TV optical unit is mounted in a pod under the nose.

The Tomcat's built-in armament consists of one General Electric M61A-1 Vulcan 20 mm gun mounted in the port side of the forward fuselage, with 675 rounds of ammunition. Main missile armament comprises four Sparrow AAMs partially recessed under the fuselage, or four Phoenix AAMs mounted below the fuselage. In addition, four Sidewinder AAMs, or two Sidewinders plus two Phoenix or two Sparrow, can be carried on two underwing pylons. The Tomcat can carry a mixture of ordnance — missiles and bombs — up to a maximum of 14,500 lb. ECM equipment includes the Goodyear AN/ALE-39 dispenser which carries and deploys chaff, flares and miniature jammers; it can operate under manual or automatic control and payloads may be ejected singly or in pre-programmed combinations, depending on the tactical situation. Another piece of ECM equipment, the Sanders Associates ALQ-100/126, is mounted in a small pod under the nose and is used for noise and deception jamming over several frequency bands.

The Tomcat's tandem cockpit stands some height above the

ground and getting into it is not easy, but once inside the pilot and weapons officer (or naval flight officer, to give him his full title) have plenty of working room. The centrepiece of the pilot's cockpit is the air combat manoeuvre panel (ACMP), which incorporates all the controls necessary for arming and controlling the weapons. A flick of a master switch throws the AWG-9 weapons control system into instant dogfight configuration. Above the panel is the headup display, with all its various modes. The pilot also has a horizontal situation display, which provides him with all the information necessary for the tactical conduct of the mission — navigational data and so on — and a vertical display indicator, which provides a running commentary on a cathode-ray tube about the aircraft's attitude in reference to its surroundings, together with data appropriate to the engagement of targets. Weapon selection and release switches are incorporated in the combined stick and throttle.

The most prominent item of equipment in the rear cockpit is the detailed data display (DDD), which provides comprehensive information on the targets tracked by the AWG-9. Below it is the tactical information display (TID) which, by means of symbols generated by the computer, gives the crew an instant picture of the tactical situation at any given moment. The pilot can call up a repeat on his horizontal situation display. The weapons officer is also responsible for operating the electronic countermeasures control panel (ECMP) and the sensor control panel (SCP) which governs the search pattern of the radar antenna. Using the Armament Control Panel (ACP) he selects the delivery mode, timing, arming and release of the Tomcat's air-to-ground weapons; under certain circumstances he can also control the launch of air-to-air weapons, although this is normally the function of the pilot.

If the alert state is high prior to launch, the Tomcat crew will remain strapped into their cockpits for anything up to two hours, with all external units plugged into the aircraft. When the order to go finally comes, the aircraft is towed to the catapult by means of an attachment on the nosewheel unit. The noseleg has a forward-facing T-bar which engages in the catapult shuttle; a weak link, attached between a holdback bar at the rear of the noseleg and a strong point on the stern end of the catapult run, is stressed to snap at a certain loading and ensures that the aircraft cannot be launched until the catapult has developed enough power to override the weak link.

With the aircraft positioned over the catapult, its weight is set on a Capacity Safety Valve by the catapult officer, who chalks the figure on a board and shows it to the pilot. The latter confirms that the weight figure is correct with a thumbs-up signal and the figure is then passed down to the catapult pressure operator, who ensures that enough steam pressure is available to handle the weight shown.

When the steam has risen to the appropriate pressure a light shows on the catapult firing panel and the blast deflectors come up behind the aircraft. The launch handling crew give the aircraft a last check to ensure that nothing is out of place, pitot covers have been removed and that the control surfaces move freely. Next, while the Tomcat's crew keep their hands visible on their helmets to show that they are out of reach of any armament switches, an armament specialist removes the weapons pylon safety pins and the armament master safety break. Another crewman plugs a cable from the carrier's SINS — Ship Inertial Navigation System — into the aircraft's INS to give it a last-minute update before take-off; SINS is fed by Loran and Omega, which govern the carrier's navigation, and two daily star shots are taken as a backup.

The catapult shuttle is attached, the launch crew clear the area and the catapult officer checks the track of the Type 13 catapult for any obstacles before signalling the pilot to open up to full power. The signal is given with a green flag; if the launch has to be aborted for any reason the catapult officer will raise a red flag, which he keeps hidden behind his back, and will keep it above his head until steam pressure has been reduced and it is safe to take the aircraft off the catapult. If the abort signal is given, PriFly — the air commander in Primary Flying Control — will hit an override that prevents all catapults except those actually in the middle of a launch from firing until the trouble is sorted out.

If everything is OK the Tomcat pilot salutes the catapult officer, who brings his green flag down to the deck in a crisp chopping motion. The catapult fires immediately, and 2.2 seconds later the Tomcat is in the air off the bow of the ship at 150 kt.

A Task Force's Tomcats are normally tasked to fly three types of mission: Barrier CAP, Task Force CAP and Target CAP. Barrier CAP involves putting up a defensive screen at a considerable distance from the task force under the direction of a Grumman E-2C command and control aircraft, which carries the General Electric APs-120/125 search and surveillance radar. Since fighters flying Barrier CAP are likely to encounter the greatest number of incoming enemy aircraft, Tomcats usually carry their full armament of six Phoenix AAMs. These weapons, which carry a 60 kg HE warhead, reach a speed of more than Mach 5 and have a range of over 125 miles, which makes them highly suitable for long-range interception of aircraft flying at all levels and also sea-skimming missiles. Hostile aircraft or missiles that survive the attentions of the Tomcats on Barrier CAP are engaged by the fighters of the Task Force CAP, which operate within sight of their ships and which are armed with a mixture of Phoenix, Sparrow and Sidewinder AAMs. If targets still show signs of breaking through and all defensive AAMs are expended, the Tomcats can continue the engagement with their Vulcan cannon at close range.

Target CAP is an escort task, with the Tomcats riding shotgun on the Carrier Air Group's strike force. For this the Tomcats' primary armament will be the medium- and close-range Sparrow and Sidewinder, backed up by the M61 cannon. In the escort role, the Tomcats usually operate in 'loose pairs', the kind of formation adopted by Kleeman and his wingman in the action described earlier.

In a close-in dogfight, the Tomcat has the advantage of being a very manoeuvrable aircraft, thanks to its automatic VG wing and also the long tunnel between the engines, which produces a lifting effect. Tomcat pilots swear blind that nothing will out-turn them except a Harrier, and Harriers do not fight fairly.

The recovery of an Air Group to its parent carrier is a complex business. A Case One recovery, which is carried out in daylight with a minimum cloudbase of 5,000 ft and a horizontal visibility of at least 5 nm, is a visual, non-radio procedure, with the recovering aircraft stacked up at various levels in the circuit awaiting their turn to land-on. The Tomcats are usually first back, slotting into a left-hand orbit around the carrier at 2,500 ft; subsequent waves of returning aircraft will be stepped up at 1,000 ft intervals.

The Tomcats with the lowest fuel margin go in first, directed by the formation leader. Each aircraft makes a pass along the starboard side of the ship and breaks downwind at 800 ft with the carrier half a mile off its port wingtip; separation between individual aircraft on the downwind leg is 45 seconds. At the end of the downwind leg the pilot flies a curved approach crosswind, entering finals at three-quarters of a mile behind the carrier and picking up the deck landing sight. This consists of a large mirror, gyroscopically mounted so that it retains its position in the vertical plane despite the pitching of the ship. The mirror has a source light shining on it, with a horizontal row of lights on either side. These are called the datum lights. The source light is white and the datum lights are coloured. During his approach the pilot can see the source light reflected in the mirror and he judges his height on the approach by the position of the reflection of the source light in relation to the datum lights. If the pilot is approaching too high, the reflection of the source light appears near the top of the mirror, and if his approach is too low the reflection appears near the bottom. When flying down the correct approach path, the reflection of the source light appears stationary in the centre of the mirror and in line with the coloured datum lights. Carrier pilots call it 'flying the ball'.

Final approach is usually flown with a sink rate of 750 ft per minute (although rates of up to 1,000 ft per minute have been used with no adverse consequences) and this is calculated to bring the Tomcat down to engage the third arrester wire. The Landing Safety Officer, positioned next to the mirror sight, monitors the approach through an optical sight and talks the pilot down the glideslope on a short-range VHF radio, issuing instructions to increase or decrease power as necessary or make corrections to keep the aircraft on the centreline. If there is a sudden deck obstacle, or if the approach is badly wrong, he will order the pilot to overshoot. The Landing Safety Officer also operates a switch which he keeps depressed while an aircraft is on the approach; this illuminates the green light that indicates a clear deck. If he removes the pressure the light turns red and the approaching pilot overshoots without further instructions.

As soon as the Tomcat hits the deck the pilot opens the throttles to full power in case he misses the arrester wires and a short take-off becomes necessary. The forces imposed on the 22-ton aircraft at the moment of impact are considerable; the main undercarriage takes an eighty-ton load, the nosewheel a thirty-ton load, each ton of stores a ten-ton load, the arrester hook a fifty-ton load and the crew a load of a ton-and-a-half. It all adds up to the Tomcat being slammed on to the deck with an impact producing about six times the energy imposed on an aircraft landing on a conventional runway. If the wire is engaged, the Tomcat comes to a dead stop from its approach speed of 134 kts in just two seconds.

If the pilot has to make repeated overshoots for any reason — three is usually the limit — he will be ordered to break off and rendezvous with an Air Group tanker aircraft, usually a KA-6D Intruder, which during flying operations is orbiting the task force at 7,000 ft five miles out from the carrier's eleven o'clock position. Having topped up his tanks he will make another approach or, in certain conditions, divert to a shore base.

A Case Two recovery is similar to a Case One, but with a reduced cloudbase of 1,000 ft. Case Three is a night or bad weather recovery which is governed either by the Automatic Carrier Landing System (ACLS) or a Carrier Controlled Approach (CCA) letdown. Using the ACLS, an aircraft can make a fully-automated approach with the pilot flying hands-off, although he can override the autopilot if necessary. Alternatively he can make an ILS approach, manually maintaining a constant angle of attack with the throttles linked to the ACLS. The radar-directed CCA approach is flown down to three-quarters of a mile, at which point the pilot takes over visually and completes his approach with the aid of the deck landing mirror and instructions from the Landing Safety Officer.

When a Case Three recovery is necessary, the first returning aircraft is directed by an E-2C Hawkeye (one of which is always on station over the task force) to a point at 5,000 ft and twenty miles astern of the carrier. Subsequent aircraft are slotted in at intervals of one mile, each aircraft being 1,000 ft higher than the one in front. Every fifth slot is kept free so that any overshooting aircraft — which have a lower fuel margin than the ones behind — can rapidly rejoin the approach for another attempt. Using this system, the average Case Three recovery rate is one aircraft per minute.

Thanks to current and planned updates, the F-14 Tomcat will remain the US Navy's primary interceptor until well into the 21st century. Substantial updating of the aircraft's systems has been made necessary by the growing sophistication of Soviet electronic warfare techniques, which no longer rely on brute-force barrage noise jamming as they did in the 1970s. If the Russians find a means of interfering with the F-14's AWG-9 weapons control system, then the Tomcat is effectively blinded.

To counter this, Grumman have developed a new generation of Tomcat, the F-14D, which will be delivered to the US Navy from 1990. At the heart of the F-14D is a new radar system, presently designated APG-XX. A digital version of the well-proven AWG-9, the APG-XX will feature monopulse angle tracking, digital scan control, target identification and raid assessment. With monopulse, the target can be located precisely within the radar beam, enabling individual targets to be sorted out from a close formation and so assist accurate raid assessment. Digital control of the antenna scan pattern enables the radar, while continuing to scan tracked targets every two seconds, to take a look at other areas as well. Analysis of the radar returns will provide IFF information without the need for interrogation. In addition, the new radar will have an advanced electronic counter-countermeasures capability by blanking out the channels through which enemy jamming signals enter the system.

As well as the radar, the F-14D will be fitted with an infra-red search and track (IRST) sensor and a television camera set (TCS) with a telephoto lens and contrast tracker for visual target identification; the latter unit has already been retrospectively fitted to the F-14A.

The 'digital' F-14D Tomcat's avionics will incorporate five databuses, one for the main computer, two for the mission computers, one for the radar and one for the armament system. A data storage set will record all information relevant to flight and mission profiles, as well as all faults and incidents connected with the aircraft's systems. For ECM, the F-14D will carry the ALQ-165 airborne self-protection jammer, which provides both deception and noise jamming against several threats at the same time and which is effective against both pulsed and continuous-wave radars.

One of the most futuristic items of equipment to be incorporated in the F-14D is JTIDS (Joint Tactical Information Distribution System), a secure, jam-resistant, high-capacity voice and datalink. JTIDS gleans tactical information — such as the position, identity and status of friendly forces, the tracks and positions of enemy forces, target assignments, intercept control and general information including weather conditions — from a network served by perhaps hundreds of users. All this information is promulgated on a single-channel network, each user being allocated a specific time at which the channel is available for his use.

JTIDS data required for transmission is encoded and fragmented by a terminal and then transmitted in a burst lasting less than eight milliseconds. The information is received by another terminal, reassembled, decoded and filtered for the data required by the user. The F-14D will be fitted with a JTIDS Class 2 terminal with 64 channels, two for voice. Because JTIDS has no master control, the system is secure against enemy action.

The F-14D will be powered by the General Electric F-110-GE-400, which is basically the same as that which powers the Air Force's

F-15 and F-16 fighters. At last, the Navy will have the engine it wants, with a dry thrust of 16,610 lb (an increase of 4,260 lb over the F-14A's TF30) and a thrust with reheat of 27,080 lb. The new engine will enable a fully-laden F-18D to be launched without reheat — something that would be suicidal with an F-14A — and guarantees a positive climb rate even if one engine fails on take-off. This ability to launch without reheat, together with thirty per cent lower afterburning fuel consumption, adds up to an increase in CAP time of 35 per cent and an intercept radius increase of no less than sixty per cent — a vital factor when countering long-range cruise missiles.

Some of the digital F-14D's avionics were originally designed for the McDonnell Douglas F-18 Hornet, which was ordered into production for the US Navy and Marine Corps in two versions: the F-18A single-seat fighter/interdictor to replace the F-4 Phantom, and the A-18A single-seat attack aircraft to replace the A-4 Skyhawk and the A-7 Corsair II. The Hornet is also being delivered to the Canadian Armed Forces, the Royal Australian Air Force and the Spanish Air Force.

Fighter F-18s are fitted with fuselage-mounted Sparrow missiles and three stores stations; the attack variant has fuselage-mounted

The fighting shape of the F-18 is clearly visible in this photograph. The first Hornets entered operational military service on 7 January 1983.

forward-looking infra-red and laser spot tracker/strike camera pods. Apart from that the two variants are identical down to software level and their roles can be changed if necessary in less than an hour.

As the Hornet is a single-seater, McDonnell Douglas have given a lot of thought to providing the pilot with as many key systems as possible while reducing his workload at the same time. The aircraft is flown head-up, with hands on throttle and stick, and the primary flight instrument is consequently the HUD, which is an integral part of the Kaiser multi-purpose cockpit display. The HUD also provides the pilot with attack steering information following lock-on or target designation by the Hughes AN/APG-65 multi-mode digital air-to-air and air-to-ground tracking radar. Further symbology can be presented on two multifunction CRT displays on which the pilot can call up radar, FLIR and weapon seeker images, stores management, radar warning, engine condition and built-in test information. A control panel immediately below the HUD governs communications, navigation, IFF, autopilot and other necessary data; its position enables the pilot to make inputs on the keyboard without having to look down in the cockpit.

The Hornet is powered by two General Electric F404-GE-400 low

A swarm of F-18 Hornet strike fighters from the US naval test and evaluation squadrons at China Lake and Point Mugu, California, in tight formation above Nevada.

bypass turbofan engines, each producing about 16,000 lb/st. They provide enough thrust to get a fully-laden F-18 off a runway at maximum fighter-escort take-off weight of 35,000 lb without reheat, and afterburning is not normally used for carrier take-offs. In fact, a Hornet pilot would only need to use reheat for combat manoeuvring under normal circumstances, which results in considerable fuel savings. Ground idling consumes no more than 650 lb per hour, the climb from sea level to a cruising altitude of 41,000 ft — which takes about eight minutes — uses 1,500 lb, and a cruising speed of 0.85M at that altitude requires 1,600 lb per hour per engine. In the fighter escort configuration, with two Sparrows, two Sidewinders, an M61 cannon and 570 rounds of ammunition, the Hornet can climb at 10,000 ft per minute and perform sustained 5 g combat manoeuvres at medium altitudes without reheat.

Progressive aerodynamic refinements during the course of development flying have endowed the Hornet with exceptional handling qualities. The aircraft is fitted with a digital fly-by-wire flight control system, and flight characteristics have been continually improved by re-programming the dual flight-control computers. Leading- and trailing-edge flaps are computer programmed to deflect for optimum lift and drag in both manoeuvring and cruise configurations, and ailerons and flaps are also deflected differentially for roll. When the Hornet pilot initiates a roll with a sideways movement of the stick, all these computerized factors are brought into play to give the aircraft a rate of roll in excess of 220° per second.

The flight control computers also enable the Hornet pilot to retain full control at high angles of attack. As the AoA increases, the computers cancel out aileron deflection, retract the trailing-edge flaps and select the leading-edge flaps fully down. Maximum lift is obtained at around 35° AoA, and wing root leading-edge extensions make controlled flight possible at angles of attack of up to 60°, although at a low airspeed this angle can lead to a deep stall which requires up to ten seconds for recovery.

Spinning the Hornet requires a good deal of effort. The pilot first of all switches the flight control computer to the spin recovery mode, then opens up the port engine to maximum afterburner and throttles back the starboard one to idle, if a right-handed spin is desired. He next applies full left aileron and full right rudder while pulling back on the stick to increase the angle of attack. Below 35° AoA, a departure warning tone sounds at a yaw rate of 25° per second, but it is usually necessary to establish a higher AoA before the aircraft will spin. The usual spinning modes are 50°–60° AoA with a 15°–50° per second yaw rate (low rate mode); 55°–90° AoA with a 20°–80° per second yaw rate (intermediate rate mode); and 75°–85° AoA with a 90°–130° per second yaw rate (high rate mode). Recovery from the low-rate spin mode requires asymmetric power, the pilot opening the throttle of the engine on the inside of the spin until it develops more power than the engine on the outside; otherwise, recovery is achieved by the pilot restoring symmetrical power and centralising the controls. In the low-rate mode it is sometimes necessary to use aileron in the recovery process, and an arrow on the pilot's head-down display tells him which way to move the stick. The arrow disappears as the yaw rate falls below 15° per second. In all cases, the Hornet usually comes out of the spin in a couple of turns.

The Hornet's AN/APG-65 digital tracking radar has three principal modes, Navigation, Air-to-Air and Air-to-Ground. The Navigation mode is normally used for take-off and cruise to the target area, providing basic flight information on the HUD as well as position updates, waypoints and so on. The radar switches to Air-to-Air mode when the pilot selects the kind of weaponry he wishes to use; at long range this will be the Sparrow AAM. His left-hand CRT display provides stores management information, and the right-hand display shows the relevant information in radar symbology necessary for a Sparrow engagement.

Meanwhile, the radar enters the range-while-search mode, scanning up to a range of 80 nm with a mix of medium and high pulse-repetition frequencies that ensure the best chance of detecting head-on, tail-on and crossing targets. If required, the pilot can select a 'velocity search' mode to increase detection range against targets known to have a high closing speed.

Below 40 nm the track-while-scan mode is used, enabling the radar to track ten targets at the same time. Eight of these are displayed to the pilot in order of priority, with information that includes altitude, Mach number and track. Information on his HUD tells the pilot when a target is within range and he switches to track mode, which provides accurate radar tracking through all target maneouvres and calls up attack steering and weapon launch information on the HUD, together with target information on the radar display. The weapon system computes launch parameters, illuminating the target by a special high pulse-rate radar mode, and a 'shoot' symbol appears on the HUD when the target is within the missile launch envelope.

The raid assessment mode is restricted to ranges below 30 nm, searching for differences in the return Doppler shift that will tell the pilot whether he is looking at a single aircraft trace or several aircraft flying in close formation. Below 20 nm his principal weapon is the AIM-9L Sidewinder; selection of this missile uncages the seeker head and slaves it to the radar's line of sight. Movement of the seeker head is displayed on the HUD, giving a visual check that the missile has acquired the right target.

At ranges of 5 nm or less the pilot can select his M61 six-barrel 20 mm cannon for close-in work. A director gunsight appears on the HUD and the radar switches to pulse-to-pulse frequency agility to provide accurate tracking and lead-angle prediction. If the radar breaks lock within 5 nm or if a higher priority target appears, the pilot can switch to one of three dogfight acquisition modes: Boresight, Vertical, or HUD. The first target detected between 500 ft and 5 nm is acquired automatically.

Boresight locks the radar along the aircraft centreline. A small circle appears on the HUD, which can be steered on to a visually acquired target. The Vertical scan pattern, bounded by lines on the HUD, can be rolled on to a turning target for automatic acquisition up to 60° off boresight. The HUD mode scans the 20° by 20° envelope bounded by the display field of view.

The M61 Vulcan cannon has a very high rate of fire, up to 7,200 rounds per minute, and has a relatively long barrel life of about 20,000 rounds. In the Hornet the gun lies along the aircraft centreline ahead of the cockpit, with the ammunition storage drum directly underneath. The revolving six-barrel arrangement accelerates the rate of fire to 6,000 rounds per minute in less than half a second. It is also effective against all but heavily-armoured ground targets.

For close-in combat, the M61 is probably the best weapon of its kind in the world. It can put a lot of shells into a small cone of airspace in a very short time, and a high rate of fire is one of the most important factors in modern air combat, where high aircraft speeds mean short bursts of fire. The gun, as well as the air-to-air missile, assures the potency of both the Tomcat and the Hornet as the duo that will form the US Navy's 'First Team' for years to come.

Chapter 6
The air superiority game

Ever since the aircraft became a viable fighting weapon, the outcome of land battles has been decided by the control of the air above them — the ability of one side to deny the airspace over the battlefield to the attacking aircraft of the other.

In the United States, the lessons of the Korean War — where Sabres and MiGs battled for supremacy in the stratosphere high over the Yalu — resulted in the new Century Series of fighters, armed with missiles and increasingly complex weapons systems for high-speed interception at great altitudes. In the late 1960s, however, the air war over Vietnam showed that the latest aircraft design had deviated from the practical lessons; speed and sophistication were no substitutes for manoeuvrability, and an all-missile armament was no substitute for guns. Aircraft like the Phantom, designed for combat at supersonic speeds, found themselves fighting nimble MiG-17s and MiG-21s in turning combats at 500 kt or less, and they had to be retrofitted with 20 mm cannon.

Discussion around an air superiority fighter to replace the F-4 Phantom began in 1965, and four years later it was announced that McDonnell Douglas had been selected as prime airframe contractor for the new aircraft, then designated FX; as the F-15A Eagle, it flew for the first time on 27 July 1972, and first deliveries of operational aircraft were made to the United States Air Force in 1973. By the middle of 1984, F-15s were in service with the 57th Fighter Weapons Squadron at Nellis AFB, the 405th Tactical Training Wing at Luke AFB, the 1st Tactical Fighter Wing at Langley AFB, the 36th Tactical Fighter Wing at Bitburg AB, West Germany, the 49th Tactical Fighter Wing at Holloman AFB, the 33rd Tactical Fighter Wing at Eglin AFB, the 18th Tactical Fighter Wing at Kadena AB, Okinawa, the 32nd Tactical Fighter Squadron at Soesterberg, Holland, and

interceptor units of Alaskan Air Command. Five squadrons in the USA are also allocated to air defence with the F-15.

Pilots converting to the F-15 are trained by the 405th Tactical Training Wing at Luke Air Force Base, which lies eighteen miles west of Phoenix in an area of semi-desert that is heavily creased by mountain ridges. Students arriving at Luke have about 250 hours total flying time, including thirty to forty hours of fast jet training on the AT-38 Talons of the 479th Tactical Training Wing at Holloman AFB, New Mexico.

Students spend four weeks of intensive ground school learning about the F-15's complex systems, ranging from the APG-63 radar to the Sperry air data computer and the aircraft's stores management system, features of the modern combat aircraft described elsewhere in this book. During the next five weeks they fly 41 sorties, interspersed with more lengthy ground school periods. The flying encompasses general handling, basic fighter manoeuvres, six intercept sorties, six periods of dissimilar air combat tactics, and consolidation of everything learned so far in the course. There is also a lot of simulator work. As the student progresses in his air combat training, F-5E aggressors come over from Nellis to give him a taste of the real thing.

The basics of air combat tactics learned by an F-15 pilot — or the pilot of any other air superiority fighter, for that matter — have remained unchanged for many years. The air fighting formula of Altitude-Speed-Manoeuvre-Fire! developed to good effect by Aleksandr Pokryshkin, Russia's second top-scoring air ace, in the Second World War still holds good. In simple terms, this means that the pilot who starts a combat with the advantage of height and speed will also have the advantage of manoeuvrability as the combat twists down to lower levels and the speed falls away. This so-called aircraft energy advantage, however, is dissipated if the combat is prolonged; in this case the aircraft which possesses the higher latent energy in the form of excess power, enabling it to accelerate and climb faster than its opponent, will gain the advantage.

The past decade has witnessed a revolution in air fighting tactics. Until recently, a fighter pilot's success and survival depended on

Opposite *The F-15 Eagle air superiority fighter represented a big step forward in combat aircraft technology and broke away from the 'missile platform' concept of the 1960s.*

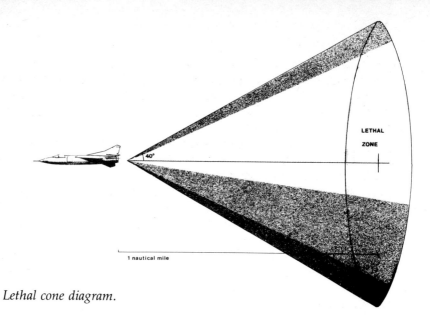

Lethal cone diagram.

his ability to keep his six o'clock clear while manoeuvring into his opponent's six o'clock in order to discharge his weapons into the so-called lethal cone, radiating at an angle of about 40° from the tail of the target aircraft and extending rearwards for a mile or so. If a pilot could keep his adversary out of this cone, the chances of the enemy aircraft getting off an effective shot with either guns or heat-seeking missiles were slim.

The 40° lethal cone theory led to the development of a number of classic air combat manoeuvres both in defence and offense. The simplest defensive manoeuvre, unchanged since Camels and Fokkers battled it out over Flanders, is the break, in which the defending pilot uses maximum g and maximum performance to turn the aircraft towards his attacker and, hopefully, cause the latter to overshoot if his closing speed is high. No matter what technical terminology it is wrapped up in today, the technique behind 'split-arsing' is the same as it was seventy years ago.

Another defensive manoeuvre is the high-g barrel roll, which depends on one's opponent having excessive closing speed and also on very accurate timing. The defending pilot watches the attacker coming in and then, at the critical moment, throttles back, extends his airbrakes and pulls his aircraft up into a barrel roll, losing speed all the time and pulling as much g as possible. The theory is that the attacker's high speed will take him through the centre of the roll, whereupon the defender completes the manoeuvre, cleans up his aircraft and increases speed to dive after his opponent, having neatly turned the tables. The problem with this evasive manoeuvre is that it has to be started at exactly the right moment; too soon, and the attacker will pull up and then dive down to hit the defending aircraft as it hangs halfway round the roll, its energy dissipated.

One of the more classic offensive combat manoeuvres is the yo-yo, which was devised by MiG pilots (probably Russians) in the later stages of the Korean War and subsequently adopted by the Americans. There are two kinds, the high-speed and the low-speed yo-yo. In the high-speed yo-yo, which is used to prevent overshooting a hard-turning target, the attacker rotates the nose of his aircraft high, aileron-turning to keep the target in sight. As his speed falls away, reducing the radius of turn at the top of the manoeuvre, he pulls hard over the top and drops down into a firing position inside his opponent's turn.

The low-speed yo-yo, on the other hand, is designed to gain the advantage over an opponent who is turning at an equal or faster rate than the attacking aircraft. The attacker enters a diving turn, gaining speed, and then rolls across the opponent's turning circle,

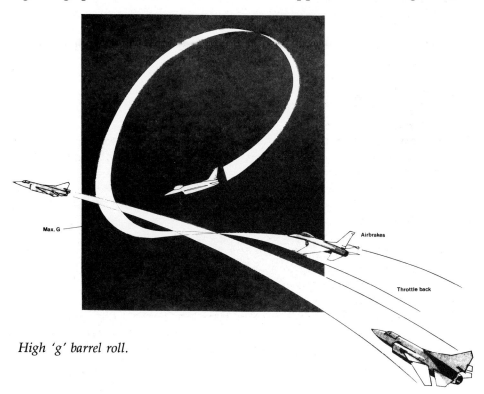

High 'g' barrel roll.

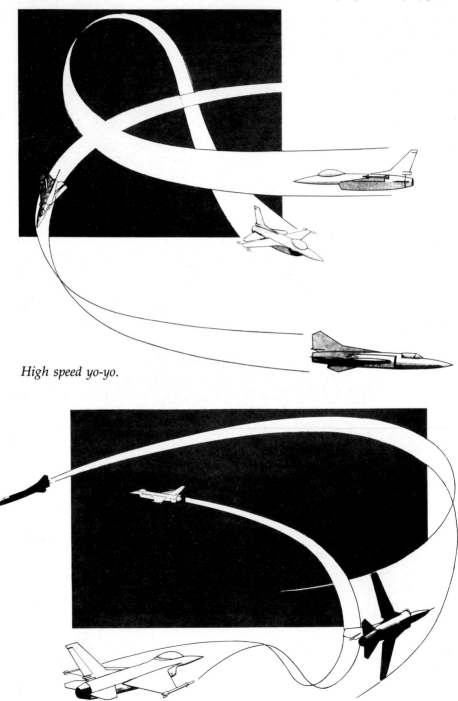

High speed yo-yo.

Low speed yo-yo.

hopefully into a firing position on the latter's tail — although by the time the manoeuvre is completed the target aircraft will have increased the distance considerably.

During the Vietnam War, American pilots flying heavy aircraft like the Phantom, which do not turn well at lower speeds, found that they had a problem when fighting lighter and nimbler aircraft like the MiG-17; in some cases, their higher speed brought them so close to the target that it reduced their weapons envelope considerably. So they developed a manoeuvre called the lag pursuit roll, in which the attacking aircraft pulls up across the target's turning circle and then rolls, dropping down into a position outside the opponent's radius of turn and about a mile astern. If the opponent keeps on turning the attacker will be in his blind spot; if the target breaks in the opposite direction he will fly across the attacker's cone of fire.

One combat manoeuvre which is still taught today, and which was developed during the Second World War, is the scissors, in which each aircraft flies as slowly as it can, continually reversing its turn in an attempt to make the opponent overshoot. It is not recommended for fighters with dissimilar manoeuvrability, because

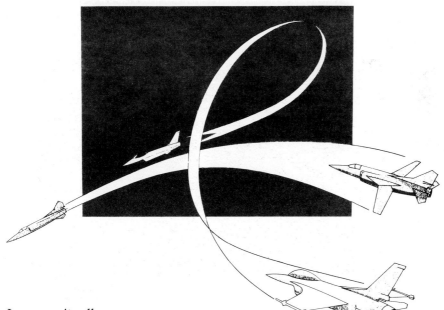

Lag pursuit roll.

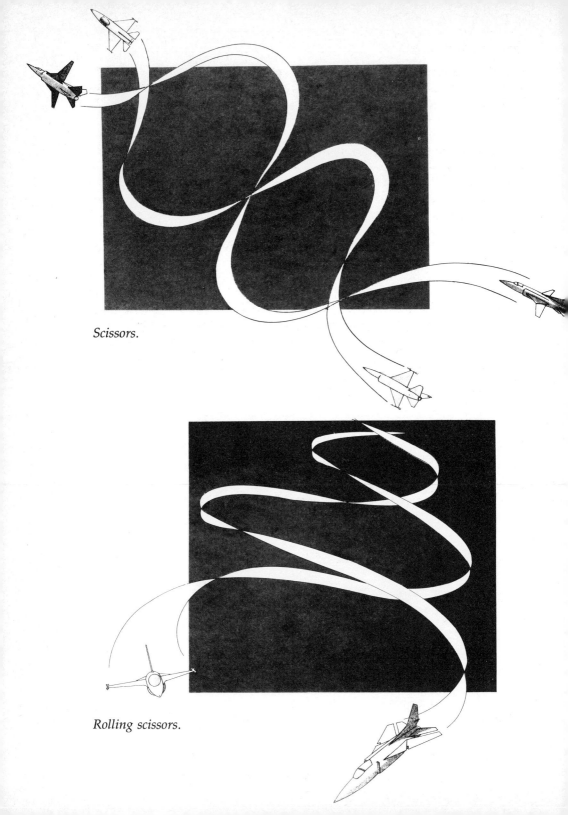

Scissors.

Rolling scissors.

the more manoeuvrable aircraft should always win. The rolling scissors is a variation in which the two opposing aircraft roll round and round one another, descending all the time. It is the ultimate game of 'chicken', because the pilot who pulls out of his dive first is dead — and if both pilots leave it too late they are both dead.

The basic fighting element of two aircraft, the pair, has remained much the same ever since the Germans perfected it during the Spanish Civil War. Today's pair of fast jets flies in line abreast, with between one and three miles between the two aircraft, and all air combat tactics are built around this basic element. On combat air patrol, the task of a pair of fighters is to locate a suspect aircraft (the Bogey), turn towards him, identify him by making a close pass, force him into a situation where his actions are predictable, and kill him.

The usual technique in a two versus one situation is for the lead aircraft of the CAP pair to make a fast head-on run towards the Bogey with his wingman some distance out to the right. As the lead pilot flashes past the Bogey at close range he makes a positive

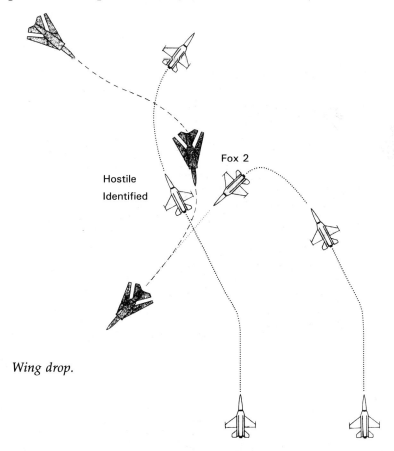

Fox 2

Hostile
Identified

Wing drop.

identification and pulls hard right astern of the enemy aircraft, whose pilot will almost certainly have dropped a wing to make his own identification. As the Bogey turns in pursuit of the aircraft that has just gone past him, the wingman will have an opportunity to get on his tail for a shot with a heat-seeking missile.

If the Bogey has detected both fighters he will probably ignore the lead aircraft as it makes its fast head-on pass and instead turn towards the number two, in which case the CAP pair will have him effectively boxed in. If the Bogey realises his mistake and reverses his turn it will put the lead CAP aircraft, which is also turning hard, in a position for a shot with a radar-guided AAM from the beam, and if he continues his turn towards the wingman the lead aircraft

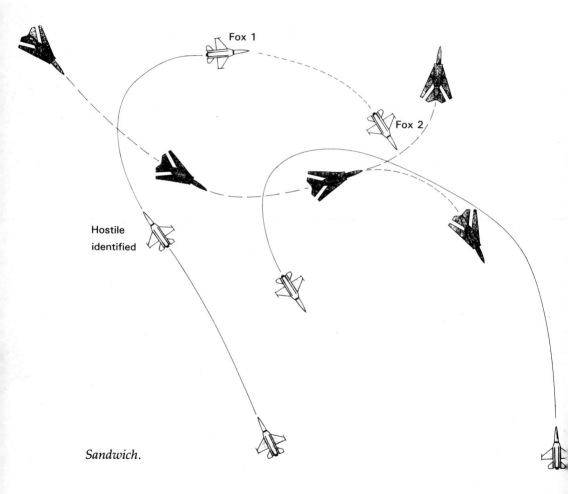

Sandwich.

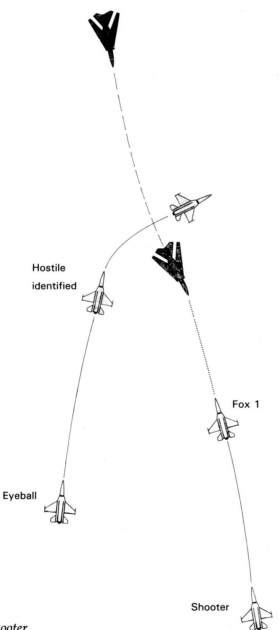

Hostile
identified

Fox 1

Eyeball

Shooter

Eyeball/Shooter.

will pull round on his tail for a heat-seeking AAM shot. If the Bogey evades this he will still have to contend with the wingman, who will pass him head-on at high speed and then turn hard to make his own attack from astern or the beam.

Another option, known as the Eyeball/Shooter, is aimed to kill the Bogey in the shortest possible time without becoming committed to a turning fight. The lead CAP fighter makes his fast head-on pass to identify the enemy aircraft, but his wingman, who is some distance astern of the leader, fires a radar-guided AAM from a direct head-on position.

In a shooting war, the aim of the Warsaw Pact air forces will be to penetrate deeply into NATO territory, striking airfields, fuel and ammunition dumps, radar sites, command centres and ports,

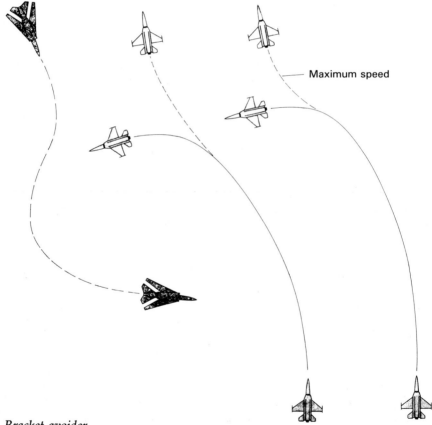

Maximum speed

Bracket avoider.

especially those handling reinforcements. Warsaw Pact air superiority fighters will patrol over the armoured forces, ready to intercept any NATO strike aircraft. The NATO air forces will already be at a disadvantage, for whereas the Warsaw Pact can allocate much of its combat strength to attack, NATO will have to divide its effort between air support and air defence.

This is not to say that the Warsaw Pact air superiority fighters would have things all their own way. A high degree of co-ordination exists among the NATO strike squadrons; to give just one small but important example, the universal language among NATO aircrew is English, but no such standardization exists in the Warsaw Pact.

The NATO strike squadrons practice their skills under realistic combat conditions during a Tactical Air Meet which is held once every two years. The exercise is highly competitive and gives participating aircrews experience of operating in a simulated high-threat environment. The first part involves attacks on ground targets at ranges in West Germany and the Low Countries by flights of four aircraft, these having to negotiate areas defended by SAMs, AAA and fighters flying CAP. Simulated attacks are also carried out on selected NATO airfields. The only drawback to the air of realism that surrounds the operation is that crews must observe strict height and speed limits to avoid disturbing the local population; except when over the target, aircraft must maintain a height of at least 500 ft and remain below 480 kt.

The second part calls for each participating crew to fly up to five sorties by day or night. On each of the daytime flights, a simulated target is set up somewhere along a non-standard route; the target has to be overflown with no more than 100 metres lateral error and within plus or minus 20 seconds of the time estimated during flight planning for points to be scored.

A typical airfield attack mission might involve a joint operation by RAF Jaguars and Luftwaffe Tornados and F-4s — say four Tornados, four Jaguars and eight Phantoms. The Tornados would go in first to hit the airfield dispersal areas (which in war would probably be very crowded) with cluster bombs, while the F-4s, attacking next in two waves, would hit hardened aircraft shelters and runways with retarded bombs. Finally, the four Jaguars, coming in fast about three miles behind the Phantoms, would pull up into a 30° climb for a toss-bombing attack, releasing their total of sixteen 1,000-lb iron bombs at an altitude of 1,500 ft. Two of the bombs would be fuzed to explode half an hour after impact, the third one hour after impact, and the fourth five hours afterwards.

The Jaguar squadrons, equipped with aircraft that are very difficult to spot when flying at low level, have worked out special tactics to cope with hostile air superiority fighters and have used them to good effect both in Europe and on Red Flag exercises. A favourite ploy is to fly in 'card' formation, with the leading pair of Jaguars flying in line abreast with up to 4,000 yd separation between the two, and the second pair fifteen seconds behind. If a CAP aircraft spots the leading pair and comes down to engage them, he will drop into the middle of the box and present the second pair with a good opportunity for a cannon shot. This technique has worked on a number of occasions against F-15s. If a fighter does get within gun range of a Jaguar at low level, the latter's best avoiding tactic is to jink, especially up and down; this creates a turbulent wake that extends a long way behind the aircraft and can seriously upset the attacker's aim.

Aircraft that can jink really well, like the A-10 Thunderbolt II, present CAP pilots with a real problem. Russia's equivalent is the Su-25 Frogfoot, and as both types use similar aggressive fighter-like tactics to counter a would-be attacker, it is worthwhile examining the A-10 in some detail.

The A-10 was born out of the Vietnam War, which revealed a serious lack of an aircraft designed specifically for ground attack and close support. The result was an aircraft of unusual appearance and quite remarkable ugliness; it quickly became known as the 'Warthog'. But the A-10 was not designed to win a beauty contest; it was built to fly low and slow and to carry a big load. Its purpose is to kill tanks, and for this its maximum speed of about 350 kt is quite sufficient.

The real beauty of the A-10 is the way it is designed to fulfil its primary mission. It is fitted with modern avionics such as a central air data computer, an inertial navigation system and a head-up display, but the aspect of its design around which everything revolves is its ability to carry the maximum firepower and continue to survive in a highly hostile environment.

The aircraft is very heavily armoured, the pilot sitting in a titanium 'bathtub', and the airframe has a built-in redundant structure policy, which means that the pilot can retain control even if large portions of the airframe are shot away. The A-10's built-in firepower is its massive GAU-8/A 30 mm seven-barrel rotary

Close-up of the Fairchild A-10's 30 mm seven-barrel rotary cannon installation.
Note the different air-cooling configuration in the two photographs.

cannon, which is mounted on the centreline under the forward
fuselage. The gun fires up to 4,200 rounds per minute of armour-
piercing ammunition with a non-radioactive uranium core for
greater impact, and is quite capable of destroying a light tank or
armoured car. The aircraft also has eight underwing and three
under-fuselage attachments for up to 16,000 lb of bombs, missiles,
gun pods and jammer pods, and carries the Pave Penny laser
system pod for target designation.

Pilots converting to the A-10 make five conversion flights
followed by a number of range sorties during which they get used
to the aircraft's weaponry. Further sorties are flown in a realistic
tactical environment, this part of the course including night flying,
and pilots round off their conversion by flying twelve sorties to
accustom them to A-10 tactics within the European environment.

Main European bases for the A-10 are Bentwaters and Woodbridge, in Suffolk, from where the 81st Tactical Fighter Wing deploys its squadrons to Forward Operating Locations in Germany. Of necessity, A-10 pilots must be more familiar with the West German countryside than anyone except helicopter crews and the RAF's Harrier Force. Aircraft usually deploy to FOLs in clutches of eight or nine; each FOL has a computer link with Bentwaters, so that when spares are needed they can be rapidly flown out, as can ground crews to undertake major servicing. This arrangement does away with the need to maintain large stocks of spares in Germany, with all the attendant need for more personnel and resulting logistics problems.

The A-10 is designed for a very high sortie rate, so servicing is made as simple as possible to cut down turnround time. Most of the aircraft's inspection panels can be reached by a man standing on the ground, and an automatic system assures rapid reload of the 1,350-round GAU-8/A ammunition drum. The fact that the 81st TFW has been known to fly 86 sorties with eleven aircraft in one day gives a good idea of the A-10's capabilities; in fact, the sortie rate limit is determined by pilot fatigue. After three sorties of high-g manoeuvring at low level, any pilot's performance begins to suffer.

The A-10s operate in two-ship flights and each pair can cover a

One of the first Fairchild A-10 Thunderbolt IIs to equip the 81st Tactical Fighter Wing at Bentwaters, Suffolk.

swathe of ground up to six miles wide. In practice, however, the best swathe width has been found to be two to three miles, so that an attack can quickly be mounted by the second aircraft once the first pilot has made his firing pass on the target. The A-10 has a combat radius of 250 nm, enough to reach a target area on the East German border from a FOL in central Germany and then move on to another target area in northern Germany. The aircraft has a three-and-a-half hour loiter endurance, although wartime sorties in Europe would probably last from one to two hours. The 30 mm ammunition drum carries enough rounds to permit ten to fifteen firing passes.

The pilot of an A-10 sits on a zero-zero Aces II ejection seat in a cockpit designed to give excellent all-round visibility. At the A-10's very low operating height, any vision obstruction can be fatal. In fact, A-10 pilots are more worried about the proximity of the ground than about AAA or CAP fighters. The A-10 is a large aircraft, and in a vertical bank the wingtip is 25 feet nearer the ground than the pilot. This presents problems when the aircraft is manoeuvring under low cloud, so when working down low pilots must learn to do level turns in the minimum radius. One of the A-10's assets is its audible stall warning device; the aircraft's stall is very docile and there is an almost complete lack of indication, so the warning device emits two sounds, one to indicate peak turning performance and the other to give warning of an incipient stall. Optimum performance comes at nine-tenths maximum lift and 21 angle-of-attack units and corresponds to a 4,000 ft diameter turning circle.

The A-10's excellent short field performance means that the aircraft can be deployed from its forward operating locations to literally thousands of unprepared strips capable of accepting one or more A-10s. With the aid of its decelerons — combined ailerons and airbrakes — the aircraft can land on a strip less than 1,500 ft long.

With uranium-core ammunition, an A-10 pilot can engage enemy armour at a range of between 6,000 and 4,000 ft; in fact, the gunsight is calibrated at the 4,000 ft range mark. This, coupled with the aircraft's turning circle of 4,000 ft, means that the aircraft can engage a target without having to pass over it. A one-second burst will place seventy rounds in the target area, and as a complete 360° turn takes no more than sixteen seconds two A-10s can bring continuous fire to bear.

The A-10's principal enemy is the Soviet ZSU-23/4 AAA, and to stand any chance of survival in a hostile environment dominated by this weapon the Warthog pilot must fly at 100 ft or less and never remain straight and level for more than four seconds. Survivability also depends on close co-operation between the two A-10s; while one engages the target, the other stands off and engages anti-aircraft installations with its Maverick TV-guided missile, six of which are normally carried on triple launchers.

If an A-10 is attacked by a hostile fighter, the standard tactic is to turn head-on towards the threat and use coarse rudder to spray the attacker with 30 mm ammunition. Su-25 Frogfoot pilots are thought to employ similar tactics, which probably makes aircraft in this class the most difficult targets of all for an air superiority fighter pilot.

So far, the modern generation of air superiority fighters has not been tested in real combat against nimble ground-attack types like the Su-25, and only one nation — Israel — has seen action with its force of F-15s and F-16s. The combat debut of Israel's F-15s came on 27 June 1979, when several aircraft of this type were escorting a mixed force of IAF Phantoms and Kfirs in an attack on Palestinian guerilla targets on the southern coast of Lebanon between Tyre and Beirut. The attacking force was intercepted by Syrian Air Force MiG-21s, which were engaged by the F-15s and the Kfirs while the Phantoms pressed home their strikes. Two separate air battles developed, each lasting between two and three minutes, and the Israelis claimed the destruction of five Syrian aircraft.

Israel's F-16s went into action for the first time on 7 June 1981, when eight aircraft made a long-range low-level precision attack on Iraq's Osirak nuclear reactor near Baghdad. The Israelis claimed that the reactor, which was then in the process of construction, was to be used for work in connection with an Iraqi nuclear weapons programme. It was scheduled to become operational in the late summer of 1981, and according to Israeli sources it would have provided Iraq with the means of producing up to five 20-kiloton atomic bombs.

Whatever the truth may have been, the Israeli Air Force was instructed to knock out the reactor and the air strike was timed to take place at 06:30 hours local time on a Sunday to minimise civilian casualties. Fighter escort for the operation was provided by six F-15s.

The aircraft took off from Etzion, near Eilat, and flight-refuelled before heading across Jordan at low level and then continuing over the barren northern territory of Saudi Arabia. The pilots reported sporadic and inaccurate anti-aircraft fire as they crossed the border into Iraq, but no further opposition was encountered during the remainder of the operation; even though the heavily camouflaged reactor site was protected by SAMs, none were launched.

The strike pilots had no difficulty in locating the target; abortive rocket attacks had been made on the site earlier by Iranian F-4 Phantoms, and Iran had been willing to provide photographic intelligence. The F-16s went in at very low level and completely destroyed the French-built 70MW reactor in an attack with Paveway

Below and overleaf *The nimble F-16 Fighting Falcon, combat-proven by the Israeli Air Force, has also proved highly popular with NATO pilots. It can deliver a formidable weapons load, then assume the role of air superiority fighter.*

2,000 lb bombs. These are laser-guided, and it is possible that the target was illuminated by an F-4 carrying a Pave Spike laser designator, but this was never confirmed by the Israelis.

In the summer of 1982, the Israeli Air Force embarked on a period of intensive action in support of the invasion of the Lebanon. Israeli and Syrian combat aircraft had been involved in a series of skirmishes over Lebanese territory since 1979, and in the course of these F-15s encountered MiG-25 Foxbats for the first time. Since the F-15 had been designed to counter the MiG-25 in the air superiority role in the first place, the results of these actions, which were firmly in the F-15's favour, attracted a lot of attention. The Israelis reported that the Foxbat was fast at high altitude but that its manoeuvrability was poor, as was the visibility from the cockpit. At medium and low altitudes the heavy MiG-25's speed fell away markedly and its handling qualities were sluggish.

The MiG-23 Flogger, according to the Israelis, was a much better proposition, but the Syrian tactics left a lot to be desired. A senior Israeli Air Force officer, speaking in an interview with *Flight International* about the summer 1982 air battles over the Bekaa Valley, said that '...The pilots behaved as if they knew they were going to be shot down and waited to see when it was going to happen and not how to prevent it, or how to shoot us down. Which was strange, because in the 1973 war the Syrians fought aggressively. This time it was different, so it was difficult to compare the aircraft. They could have flown the best fighter in the

Command and control aircraft like the E-2 Hawkeye are indispensible to modern air warfare; this type was used to good effect by the Israeli Air Force in combat over the Bekaa Valley.

world, but if they flew it the way they were flying, we would have shot them down in exactly the same way. It wasn't the equipment at fault, but their tactics. Look at the area of operations and the restrictions we had. We couldn't enter Syria. They were only two minutes from their bases, while we were between ten and forty minutes from base; some of our aircraft had to come from Ouvda down in the Negev. Most of the kills, 85 to 90 per cent, were in the Bekaa Valley, less than a minute from the Syrian border. It meant we only had two minutes from them crossing to crossing back if they only wanted to sweep the Bekaa area. If we didn't succeed in two minutes then we couldn't follow them across the border. That was a difficult situation for us. Maybe for them as well.... They fired missiles, they fought, but in a peculiar way. I didn't mean they were sitting ducks, but in our view they acted without tactical sense. Maybe in their view the best tactic was to get away from — I don't know what. But the results show it was very strange; we're still trying to assess what they were trying to do.'

Israel invaded the Lebanon on 4 June 1982 and the first Syrian loss occurred on 7 June, when a MiG-25R Foxbat was destroyed during a high-level reconnaissance mission. The Israelis have always refused to say what shot it down, but it was probably one or more F-15s armed with Sparrow AAMs. Four more MiGs (MiG-21s or -23s or both) were shot down on the following day, but the major air battle over the Bekaa started on 9 June, when Israeli A-4 Skyhawks, F-4 Phantoms and Kfirs launched the first big attacks on Syrian SAM and artillery sites east of Beirut. It was the first time the Kfir had been in action and a superlative aircraft it proved to be, both in the air-to-ground and air-to-air roles.

During the air fighting that accompanied the invasion of southern Lebanon the Israelis claimed to have shot down 92 Syrian fighters, about half of them MiG-23 Floggers. (This claim was seriously disputed, and in fact there is some evidence that Israeli claims are not always as accurate as they might be.) Forty aircraft were claimed to have been shot down by F-15s and 44 by F-16s, Phantoms and Kfirs accounting for the handful of others.

Air-to-air missiles used by the Israelis were predominantly the AIM-9L Sidewinder and the Rafael Shafrir Mk 2, with a smaller proportion of Sparrows and Rafael Python 3. The Python, which has since replaced the Shafrir on the production line, is a passive infra-red homing weapon using a single-element cooled infra-red detector with a gimbal angle of plus or minus 30°. This can be

Air superiority nowadays depends on adequate warning of low-level attackers: pictured is one of six Boeing AWACs aircraft assigned to NATO.

operated in boresight, uncaged or radar-slaved mode and permits attacks from all aspects.

The Sparrow AAM was used only within visual range and the Israelis reported that of all the AAMs used, the Shafrir was the most effective. One surprising aspect of the Bekaa air combats was the high percentage of gun engagements and associated kills; this was because the combat took place in a restricted block of airspace occupied by a lot of aircraft, which meant that pilots had to get in close to the opposition to make positive visual indentification. The result was a series of classic dogfights, and it is quite probable that a similar situation would develop in NATO airspace if it ever came to a shooting war with the Warsaw Pact.

In the Yom Kippur war of 1973, the Israeli Air Force had been unable to establish air superiority over the west bank of the Suez Canal because of the high density of modern Egyptian SAM sites and radar-controlled AAA. Of the 102 Israeli aircraft lost in that conflict, 39 were shot down by SAMS, and AAA accounted for the rest. (The Egyptians, incidentally, also shot down 45 of their own aircraft.) During the invasion of the Lebanon, therefore, SAM and AAA sites were singled out for high-priority air attacks at an early stage. The Israeli strike aircraft used electronic warfare and deception techniques to get through to the sites, which were destroyed one by one from very low level with 'iron' bombs. Many of the batteries were knocked out as they were being moved from one site to another and were consequently vulnerable to air attack;

the Syrians had relied on fighter CAP to defend their weapons during the mobile phase and committed large numbers of aircraft, hoping to establish air superiority by weight of numbers; in fact, the air superiority scales were tilted the other way because of the better skill and tactics of the Israeli pilots.

The F-15 and F-16 are the first American aircraft capable of dogfighting in the true sense of the word since the F-86 Sabre. As stated earlier, the philosophy behind the design of the Century-Series fighters, although it seemed sound at the time, proved

The Lockheed F-104 Starfighter, seen here in prototype TF-104 two-seater guise, was designed as an interceptor and finished as a low-level multi-role aircraft for NATO, carrying out tasks for which it was never intended.

eventually to be false; they were heavy and unwieldy weapons platforms rather than fighters, and were only capable of manoeuvring well at supersonic speeds.

The F-104 Starfighter was a classic example. Originally designed as a pure high-speed interceptor, it was eventually adapted (mainly for political reasons) as a multi-role aircraft for NATO as the F-104G, carrying stores it was never designed to lift, to the consequent detriment of both airframe and performance.

In the interceptor role for which it was intended, carrying two Sidewinder AAMs and an M61 Gatling gun with 725 rounds, the F-104 weighs in at 20,800 lb and its 15,950 lb/st J79 engine provides it with excellent acceleration; the initial rate of climb is 50,000 ft per minute and the limiting speed of 2.0M/750 kt IAS is easily attained

in level flight. The aircraft's tiny, razor-sectioned wing, spanning only 22 ft, imposes severe limitations on its turning performance at subsonic speeds, but once supersonic the positive g limit of 7.33 can be achieved with comparative ease at all but very high altitudes.

In the bomber and reconnaissance roles, however, the F-104G's all-up weight goes up to 27,000 lb, including over 4,000 lb of external stores. The range of the aircraft at low level with four external fuel tanks is around 600 nm at 530 kt IAS. Avionics include a Litton LN3 inertial navigator, and ground-mapping radar with offset capability to permit all-weather navigation and strike.

The Starfighter's cockpit is well laid out, with good pilot visibility and everything in easy reach. The flight controls are of the conventional powered variety — ailerons, rudder and slab tailplane — and additional aileron and rudder travel is available for low-speed handling when the undercarriage is lowered. (Many of the much-publicized accidents to Luftwaffe and RNethAF Starfighters, in fact, resulted from loss of control during the critical landing phase.) The aircraft is fitted with an automatic pitch control system which provides for artificial stall warning and avoidance; aerodynamic pre-stall warning buffet occurs over a wide IAS band depending on the aircraft's configuration (for example, at 83 per cent power, with 5,000 lb of fuel, flaps up and carrying only underwing tanks, flying straight and level, the pre-stall buffet is first experienced at 325 kt IAS) and excessive angles of attack produce pitch-up, which in turn leads to spinning from which recovery is unlikely. The pitch control system brings a stick-shaker and kicker into play when pre-set angles of attack or rates of pitch change are reached.

On the ground the Starfighter is steered by the nosewheel, which remains effective at speeds of up to 100 kt during the take-off run. In a clean configuration the aircraft unsticks at 188 kt after a roll of 2,700 ft, but with four full drop tanks the unstick speed is 213 kt after a roll of 4,600 ft. Once airborne and at cruising speed the Starfighter is stable, but manoeuvring requires heavy stick forces. It is in no sense an aerobatic aircraft; a loop with maximum dry power, started at 500 kt IAS, needs a good 10,000 ft of sky before it is completed.

The Starfighter has electrically-operated leading- and trailing-edge flaps which are blown when the LAND position is selected, using high-pressure air from the engine compressor. With flaps in the LAND position the threshold speed is between 175 and 205 kt, depending on fuel weight, and if the TAKE-OFF setting is selected the threshold speed is between 195 and 225 kt. The wheel brakes are very effective and the brake parachute can be deployed at speeds of up to 205 kt IAS to provide rapid deceleration.

Although the F-104G (and the Italian variant, the F-104S) remained in NATO's front line for many years, performing a variety of roles — for some of which it was never intended — very well indeed, one aircraft could have performed the air defence role very much better. Like the Starfighter, the English Electric (later BAC) Lightning was developed as a supersonic interceptor, but it had none of the Starfighter's limitations; in fact the Lightning was the world's only supersonic pure *fighter* aircraft until the advent of the F-15, and by the time the latter flew in prototype form the Lightning had already been in RAF service for twelve years.

When the Lightning was introduced to the RAF in the summer of 1960 it represented a leap of 100 per cent in performance over its predecessor in what was then Fighter Command, the Hunter F 6. Pilots coming to it from the latter aircraft were impressed by its apparent immense size, accentuated by the need to climb a ten-foot ladder before entering the cockpit. The cockpit and its associated equipment provided revelations too, and in some ways it was simpler than the Hunter's. For a start a personal equipment connector was used to connect the pilot to oxygen, g-suit air, air ventilated suit supply and R/T lead in a single easy operation, while the newly-designed combined seat and parachute harness made strapping-in a lot simpler. The height of the ejection seat itself could be adjusted by operating an electric switch.

The most revolutionary change in cockpit instrumentation was the elimination of the traditional artificial horizon and compass; instead, the Lightning was equipped with a master reference gyro that fed electrical signals continuously through 360° in azimuth, pitch and bank. These signals were in turn fed to an attitude indicator which indicated pitch and bank, and to a heading indicator which showed direction. The master reference gyro also supplied information to the radar fire control system and the automatic pilot. The altimeter was different, too, being a new electrically-operated design with a simplified presentation by counters appearing in small windows to indicate the altitude. A single hand swept the dial every 1,000 ft, and since the Lightning's initial climb rate was in excess of 50,000 ft per minute, the hand rotated at over 50 rpm.

The powerful Lightning F 6 is still a fine interceptor, but is costly to operate and lacks endurance. Here, two aircraft of No 11 Squadron, RAF Binbrook, are seen refuelling from a Victor tanker of No 55 Squadron.

The throttles controlling the Lightning's two Avon engines were on the left-hand cockpit console, together with what looked like a third throttle but which in fact was the controller for the AI radar scanner. Operating the AI needed some dexterity, because it incorporated twelve separate functions all of which had to be actioned by the pilot's left hand. High pressure fuel cocks were incorporated in the first movement of the throttle levers, and two switches controlled the electric low pressure cocks and eight booster pumps. Four stages of reheat could be selected at the forward end of the throttle quadrants.

The flying controls were fully powered, irreversible and supplied with artificial 'feel' which was felt as a progressive stick force as the speed increased to 0.9M, after which the stick force remained constant. If he so wished, the pilot could cut out the artificial feel by throwing a switch. Two panels, one on either side of the cockpit, contained the necessary 'doll's eyes' and warning lights, together with a prominent red warning light. This was linked to a bell which sounded in the pilot's headset, and the nature of the emergency would be shown on the standard warning panel as soon as the visual/audio warning signal was triggered. Minor emergencies or system failures were indicated on an auxiliary warning panel on the right side of the cockpit.

The Lightning's engine instruments were standard, with the rpm gauges calibrated from zero to 100 per cent. Indicators showed the position of the variable jet pipe nozzles. Starting the engines was a simple procedure and the pre-take-off vital actions could be completed very quickly, enabling the aircraft to be scrambled in a very short time. After lining up on the runway, take-off procedure was to hold the aircraft on the brakes and increase power to 85 per cent; the pilot felt an increase in air pressure as the cockpit pressurised, then released the brakes and opened the throttles to 100 per cent power. During the roll, a number of checks were made — jet pipe minimum and maximum temperatures, nozzles closed, fire warning lights out — and at 170 kt a slight backward pressure on the control column was sufficient to raise the nosewheel. A further slight increase in pressure at 170 kt caused the Lightning to unstick.

For a pilot new to the Lightning, one immediately noticeable aspect of take-off was the high nose-up attitude and the inertia that took the aircraft on a flight path parallel with the ground for some distance at unstick, giving a slight negative g or sinking sensation. However, acceleration after unstick was rapid, the speed building up to 400 kt at which point a further slight backward pressure on the stick established a climbing angle of 22° on the attitude indicator. Optimum climbing speed was 450 kt. (It is interesting to compare this with the F-15's optimum climb performance of 250 kt at a 65–70° climbing angle, giving a rate of climb of 33,000 ft per minute.) The Lightning's angle of climb was quite steep and pilots had to guard against a tendency to lower the nose, when it was quite easy to exceed 1.0M in the climb. When levelling off, the throttles had to be moved back quickly to 85 per cent power in order to keep the aircraft subsonic.

Early Lightning F Mk 1s suffered from a very limited endurance, and a flight refuelling probe was incorporated in the F Mk 1A and F Mk 2. A large ventral tank was fitted to the F Mk 6 to further improve its endurance, particularly in the overseas deployment role. All marks of Lightning, however, guzzled fuel at an alarming rate; an F Mk 3, with a maximum fuel facility of 1,200 gal, would

The 1957 Defence White Paper left the English Electric Lightning as the RAF's last all-British interceptor and the only operational British aircraft to have flown at Mach 2. Seen here are two Mk 53s of the Royal Saudi Air Force.

burn 20 gal per minute in the cruise and this would rise to 200 gal per minute in a climb with full afterburner. Despite this shortcoming, pilots were enthusiastic about the Lightning's tremendous reserve of power; towards the end of a sortie, with most of the fuel used up and the aircraft light, there was more thrust available in reheat than the weight plus drag, enabling the aircraft to climb vertically in the classic end-of-display manoeuvre that has thrilled many an air-show crowd. A full reheat climb would take the Lightning to 30,000 ft in a little under two minutes, and even in cold power it was capable of reaching the tropopause in

between three and four minutes from the start of the take-off roll.

Handling at all altitudes was good, only half control column deflection being needed to provide enough aileron movement for a fast rate of roll. Full control column displacement could be used to overcome any wing drop that might be experienced when operating at low IAS, say on final approach. Rolling manoeuvres in the transonic speed range were completely smooth, with no buffeting when accelerating or decelerating through 1.0M. At 2.0M a slight buzz of vibration, induced by the air intake, was experienced, but this had no effect on the aircraft's performance.

Landing the Lightning presented no special problems. A straight-in radar-controlled letdown to base was usually started from 48 miles out; when radar control had the returning aircraft in contact the pilot was instructed to change channels by GCI and the

The potency of today's long-range interceptor is symbolized by the Tornado F 2, which is capable of loitering on station for several hours and of engaging multiple targets simultaneously.

letdown was controlled by the radar controller until GCA established contact. The final eighteen miles of the approach was flown using ILS or GCA.

In a standard visual approach, airbrakes could be used throughout the circuit and landing to reduce the airspeed and provide more positive speed control. Final approach was begun at 190 kt, with the speed tapering off to 165 kt over the threshold and about 155 kt on touchdown. The brake parachute was streamed when the nosewheel was on the ground at 150 kt, and the aircraft could be stopped easily in less than 2,000 yd.

Although designed as a high-altitude missile-armed interceptor, the Lightning had a sturdy airframe and good low-level handling qualities that made it readily adaptable to the ground-attack role. The Lightning F Mk 53, developed for service in Saudi Arabia and Kuwait, could carry two 1,000 lb HE bombs or 36 SNEB 68 mm rockets in two packs, in addition to 44 2-in rockets in the front fuselage packs and two 30 mm Aden guns in the ventral pack. A further version proposed by BAC, but never adopted, would have enabled the aircraft to carry more than 400 different combinations of stores, including six 1,000 lb bombs or 144 SNEB rockets. Using a special pack, the Lightning could also have been employed for supersonic high- or low level reconnaissance.

However, the aircraft continued to suffer from a limited radius of action at low level, a problem that was highlighted when two squadrons were deployed to NATO's central front in Germany, where its main task was to provide defence against low-flying targets. In this role it was seldom able to use its high rate of climb or supersonic performance, and engagements were with cannon rather than missiles. A further drawback was that all-round visibility from the cockpit was poor. Nevertheless, it could out-turn anything except the Harrier, and the Lightning's rapid acceleration enabled the pilot to select an opportune moment for attack or to disengage without penalty.

In short, the Lightning admirably fulfilled a close-combat role that was far removed from its original conception. The fact that it performed that role just as well as the present generation of air superiority fighters, in many respects, remains a lesson in adaptability.

Chapter 7
The F-111: An aircraft for all seasons

On 17 March 1968, six General Dynamics F-111A fighter-bombers arrived at Takhli Air Base in Thailand on an experimental deployment known as Combat Lancer. At that time the radical variable-geometry F-111 was only part of the way through its USAF evaluation programme, and the Air Force was keen to learn how the type would shape up in a hostile environment.

Six years earlier, in 1962, the General Dynamics Corporation, in association with Grumman Aircraft, had been selected to develop a new variable-geometry tactical fighter to meet the requirements of the USAF's TFX programme. An initial contract was placed for 23 aircraft, including eighteen F-111As for the USAF and five F-111Bs for the US Navy. Powered by two Pratt & Whitney TF30-P-1 turbo-fan engines, the prototype F-111A flew for the first time on 21 December 1964, and during the second flight on 6 January 1965 the aircraft's wings were swept through the full range from 16° to 72.5°.

One hundred and sixty production F-111As were built, the first examples entering service with the 4480th Tactical Fighter Wing at Nellis AFB, Nevada, in October 1967, and it was a detachment of aircraft from this unit that made an operational deployment to Thailand in March the following year.

Operation Combat Lancer was scarcely an unqualified success. Combat sorties over North Vietnam began on 25 March, and three days later an F-111 failed to return. A second aircraft went missing on 30 March, and a third on 27 April. There were no indications as to what had happened to the first two machines, apart from the fact that they did not appear to have been lost through enemy action. The third crew, however, ejected and was picked up; the wreckage of their F-111 had fallen in friendly territory and was subjected to a thorough examination. It revealed that a control rod had suffered fatigue and snapped at a welded joint, causing the port tailplane to deflect to its maximum; this in turn had caused uncontrollable roll and pitch-up. Only a matter of days later, the same thing happened to another F-111, this time at Nellis. The three remaining Combat Lancer F-111s were hurriedly withdrawn.

Further technical problems, this time involving structural failure of the VG wing pivots — which led to the prolonged and exhaustive non-destructive testing of every F-111 in service — prevented the type's return to combat until September 1972, when the 429th and 430th Tactical Fighter Squadrons deployed to Takhli from Nellis. They were flying their first operational sorties within hours of their arrival, and the dismay at Takhli may well be imagined when one of the first two aircraft sent out failed to return. No one ever found out what happened to it, but the likeliest cause of its loss was the failure of the terrain-following radar.

On 23 October 1972, when it appeared that peace talks in Paris might lead to an agreement that would end the protracted and costly war, the United States called a halt to air operations above the 20th Parallel. Soon afterwards, however, negotiations became bogged down amid indications that the North Vietnamese were about to resume their offensive in the south. The reaction of President Richard Nixon's administration was to order the launching of the heaviest aerial assault north of the 20th Parallel so far; code-named Operation Linebacker II, it involved nearly 2,000 sorties in the space of eleven days by F-105s, F-4s, B-52s and F-111s against targets which had previously been on the restricted list. They included railway yards, power stations, communications, air defence radars, the docks at Haiphong, POL stores and ammunition dumps, together with the North Vietnamese Air Force's principal bases.

The North Vietnamese defences were terrifying. Attacking crews had to contend with surveillance radars on every piece of high ground along their approach routes, and with AAA and SAM sites dotted everywhere on the plains. During the eleven-day period of Linebacker II the enemy launched almost 1,000 SAMs and used up most of their remaining stocks of AAA ammunition in putting up what was possibly the most fearsome barrage in the history of air warfare; even so, the defences accounted for only 26 aircraft, and fifteen of those were vulnerable B-52s flying at high altitude.

The low American loss rate was due in the main to effective electronic countermeasures. By 28 December 1972 the enemy defences had been all but obliterated, and during the last two days of the campaign B-52s flew over Hanoi and Haiphong without being engaged by SAMs or fighters.

This last major air offensive led directly to the resumption of peace talks and to ceasefire negotiations which ultimately brought an end to the fighting in February 1973. The F-111, six of which had been lost in highly-defended areas since the type returned to Thailand in September, had played a vital part in the offensive — so vital, in fact, that all but the sketchiest details of the aircraft's achievements remain classified to this day.

All F-111 operations over Vietnam were flown at night, the aircraft carrying either Mk 82 500 lb bombs or Mk 84 2,000 lb bombs. The normal flight profile called for a descent to low level over Laos, then a terrain-following flight to the target area, which was usually along the railroad running north-east from Hanoi. The return flight was also made at low level until the aircraft reached Laotian territory.

In 1972 the F-111 was the most sophisticated interdictor in the world, and one moreover which had defied all its early critics to become a key weapon in the West's arsenal. To describe a low-level flight in this extraordinary machine is something that pulls the writer's ingenuity to full stretch, as will be seen from this extract from an article written by the American aviation author Ernest K. Gann, who flew in an F-111A in 1971:

'As you sink down from the heights, the mountains become ever more imposing and you remember a wager made the night before. If during the TFR run you manage to resist reaching for the stick and taking over from the automatic pilot, you will win two martinis... here are the 11,000 ft mountains approaching from directly ahead at a mere 553 miles per hour and you are looking *up* at them from the vantage of 200 ft. You indulge in some erratic swallowing and glance furtively at Wheeler [Colonel Tom Wheeler, Chief of F-111 Acceptance at Fort Worth] who is not looking out at all but is thoughtfully studying an old aviation chart, vintage 1935... As if cushioned softly against the face of a mountain, the One-Eleven rises with the slope... There is a saddle in the mountain ahead... trees higher than eye level, rocks, boulders, great chunks of very abrasive substance off both wing tips. Wheeler reaches for a knob. ''Do you prefer your ride to be soft, medium or hard?'' Your hand is curved like the talons of an eagle exactly one half inch ahead of the stick... The One-Eleven slips through the saddle and starts down the backside of the mountain, still at 200 ft and just under the speed of sound... Just as you are resigned to continuing straight through the bottom of the valley on the direct route to Peking, the autopilot levels the nose and you slither across the rumpled surface like a giant manta ray seeking food.'

The F-111's two-man crew sit side-by-side in an air-conditioned and pressurized cabin; the portion of the canopy over each seat is hinged on the aircraft centreline and opens upwards. Early aircraft had conventional ejection seats, but from No. 12 onwards F-111s were fitted with a zero-speed, zero-altitude emergency escape module developed by McDonnell Douglas and using a 40,000 lb/st rocket motor. The emergency escape procedure, which can also be initiated when the aircraft is under water, calls for both crew members to remain in the capsule cabin section, which is propelled away from the aircraft by the rocket motor and lowered to the ground by parachute. Air bags cushion the impact and form flotation gear in the event of an over-water escape, while the entire capsule forms a survival shelter.

The self-contained escape module provides a great deal more than the usual degree of crew comfort; the absence of ejection seats means that there is no complex strapping-in process. In addition, all knobs, switches and keyboards are readily to hand, and there is plenty of stowage space for maps and other documents. The only real drawback is the pilot visibility, which is poor; the pilot must rely on his systems to alert him to any threat approaching from a 60° cone to the rear, and on his weapon system officer's eyes to check the sky to starboard. Since the F-111's primary mission is low-level interdiction at night or in bad weather, however, this is not a serious shortcoming, as the aircraft depends on jamming and deception for its survival.

The F-111's engines may be started pneumatically or with a cartridge, and there is a cross-bleed starting system similar to the Tornado's. The aircraft tends to roll a little during taxi-ing because of the narrow-track undercarriage, but once it accelerates on its take-off run this disappears and the aircraft is stable. Take-off performance depends on the variant and its loaded weight; the FB-111A, for example, is the heaviest of the lot, with a maximum take-off weight of 122,000 lb. This version was developed as a bomber and missile platform for Strategic Air Command and carries either short-range attack missiles or B43, B61 or B77 free-falling nuclear bombs in its weapons bay. The thrust/weight ratio is

An F-111B with flaps down, undercarriage extended and wings swept fully forward demonstrates its low-speed handling characteristics.

considerably lower than that of other F-111 variants, but this handicap is cancelled out by the fact that the FB-111A invariably operates from very long SAC runways.

Apart from the FB-111A and the original F-111A Tactical Air Command model, other variants in service are the F-111C version for the Royal Australian Air Force; the F-111D with improved digital avionics; the F-111E with an improved stores management system and redesigned inlets; the F-111F with improved digital avionics and uprated TF30-P-100 turbofans; and the EF-111A tactical electronic warfare platform. The F-111B, the version proposed for the US Navy, was cancelled in 1968.

An F-111A in light configuration will take off in about 4,000 ft under the maximum power of both engines — a combined 36,000 lb/st. The nosewheel comes off the runway at about 140 kt and unstick speed is 160 kt. Once safe flying speed is reached and the gear is retracted, the aircraft accelerates rapidly in the climb; in fact it is not difficult to exceed 2.0M on the way up. Cleaning the aircraft up, however, seems to take longer than with other combat types; the oleos extend for a considerable length as the machine starts to get airborne, so as a safety measure the pilot must ensure that the F-111 is well clear of the runway before retracting. After that the flaps and slats are retracted, but once all this is done the F-111 comes into its element and handles exceptionally well throughout its considerable speed range.

At high level the F-111's maximum speed is in the region of 2.5M, but nobody has ever pushed the aircraft to its limits in this respect because it has a limiting skin temperature, and when this is approached a red warning light signals to the pilot that it is time to throttle back. If he fails to do so within five minutes the skin could heat to a degree where structural failure might occur. Super-sonically, the aircraft is very stable at all altitudes, including very low level, despite the sizeable shock wave its bulk produces. One pilot has described how, while watching an F-111 making a supersonic bomb run along a desert valley bombing range, he saw the entire valley floor instantly erupt in a cloud of boiling dust as the One-Eleven's supersonic shock wave struck it.

The F-111 exceeds 1.0M with its wings swept at an angle of 45°, and this is increased to 72.5° at 1.7M. Sweep angle for cruising flight is 26°. For a large airframe the F-111 is remarkably manoeuvrable at supersonic speed and will roll and turn without effort at 1.8M.

Landing the aircraft is uncomplicated, although for the best results things have to be done in strict sequence. Initial approach is made at 350 kt IAS and the speed is progressively reduced until the

In the transition to supersonic flight the F-111 brings its wings back towards the tail to give remarkable high-speed performance.

aircraft joins the circuit with the throttles at idle setting and the angle-of-attack indicator showing 10°; this is simpler to monitor than the ASI. Throttle idle setting is maintained on the downwind leg; the undercarriage is lowered and the slats and flaps extended, and the main gear landing door acts as a speed brake. The roll onto base leg is made with a sedate angle of bank of about 30°, which hardly falls into the fighter-type approach category, and power is once again applied. The F-111 has a high sink rate and its turbofan engines a correspondingly slow acceleration, so the pilot needs to have power readily available on final approach. As the aircraft approaches the runway threshold it runs into ground effect, which tends to reduce the optimum 10° angle of attack, so the pilot eases back slightly on the stick to counter this. The approach is usually flown with the wings swept fully forward at an angle of 16°, although the aircraft may be flown round the pattern with them at the 25° angle, and touchdown speed is about 140 kt. As soon as the throttles are pulled back to idle on touchdown, wing spoilers pop out to kill any remaining lift and produce further drag. The F-111 has no brake parachute, but its landing run is less than 3,000 ft and it has no trouble in getting into short strips.

F-111s form ten per cent of the USAF's tactical fighter force, but their effectiveness is greatly multiplied during night or bad weather operations. In a NATO Reforger exercise in Europe, F-111s were tasked to complete 194 sorties, thirty per cent of the total number of missions flown by participating US fighters. In the event, poor weather cut the number of F-111 sorties to 66, but even so this represented 64 per cent of the actual missions flown by all aircraft. Of these sorties, 145 were judged to have been effective — a staggering 86 per cent of the successful missions flown by all US fighters.

One area in which the F-111 scores over other contemporary types is range, which is over 3,300 nm with maximum internal fuel. In practical terms, this means that the aircraft can cross the Atlantic non-stop, without flight refuelling, on internal fuel only. In fact, the F-111's internal fuel load weighs more than a fully-laden F-16. Look at the combat radius figures in comparison with other aircraft. The F-4E Phantom, which formed the bulk of the USAF attack force in 1985, has a 250 nm radius of action with a 6,000 lb bomb load. Over the next few years the F-4s will be replaced by F-16As, which have a 350 nm combat radius with a 6,000 lb bomb load. By the 1990s, the USAF plans to operate all-weather F-15Es or F-16Es, which will be able to carry that 6,000 lb war load over a 600 nm radius. The F-111, can already carry 6,000 lb of bombs over a combat radius of 1,000 nm, and can lift its maximum war load of 24,000 lb to 350 nm.

Winding up the F-111 for a sortie is a lengthy process. The crew arrive at the aircraft a good hour before take-off, and after carrying out the external checks and strapping in there are still 45 minutes left when the engines are started. A typical training sortie will include an hour of high-level cruise, half an hour of low-level practice, with fifteen minutes or so spent in dropping practice bombs or illuminating targets by radar, and high-level cruise back to base. On arrival, depending on fuel state, the crew might spend half an hour carrying out landing approaches under various conditions. After a sortie lasting about three hours, it will take another hour to park the aircraft, shut down and go through a maintenance debriefing, and this is followed by another hour of flight debriefing and associated paperwork. So the mission, including ground time, will have lasted six hours in all.

The F-111 was the first operational aircraft in the world to have a fully automatic terrain-following radar, and therefore became the first to have a true low-level night and all-weather attack capability. It was one that imposed an entirely new challenge on the crews selected to fly the first F-111s, men at the peak of their profession. So complex is the F-111 and its systems that it takes a qualified pilot a solid year's training before he is classed as mission ready, and another year before he is fully at ease with the machinery around him. As one WSO put it:

'We earn our keep by carrying substantial payloads at high subsonic cruise speeds, at low altitudes and in any weather, deeper into enemy territory than other non-strategic aircraft could ever imagine. Cruising at eight miles a minute, 500 ft off the ground, is exciting and beautiful. You're low enough to get a really good look at the countryside, and in the United Kingdom that's rugged coastlines, lakes, mountains and castles. After a while, 500 ft seems quite high — you can get comfortable there, at least in daylight.

'On the other hand, 200 ft never seems high — it's an incredible thrill, but one you never take for granted, especially when approaching the speed of sound. The sensation of speed is amazing, and if the pilot decides to convert all that airspeed into altitude, your altimeter can read 15,000 ft in about twenty seconds! There's not a ride in a carnival anywhere that comes close to it.

'Terrain following, or 'TF-ing', is what set the F-111 in a class by itself for more than a decade. The ability to fly as low as 200 ft AGL at as fast as 1.2 times the speed of sound in almost any weather is of great tactical significance — not to mention scary! Flying at 1,000 ft AGL in mountainous terrain at night, while seeing nothing but the hazy grey/black of the inside of a cloud, punctuated only by the occasional red flash of the rotating beacon, is guaranteed to focus your attention on the task at hand, which is ensuring that the automatic TF system is working properly.

'Basically, what happens is that the TF antenna nods up and down, scanning a narrow sector in the aircraft's flight path to determine terrain elevation. This information is processed and transmitted to the flight control system which adjusts the aircraft's pitch attitude to avoid the ground. It's up to the pilot to make any necessary power adjustments. The actual path across the ground is determined by the points set into the navigational computers. Even though the aircraft has the ability to avoid the terrain in its path, it's up to the crew to plan a flight path which best uses the terrain to mask the airplane from enemy defences.

'During TF flight the atmosphere on board becomes very businesslike, the smalltalk ceases and we each monitor our instruments to make sure everything is working as intended. The commentary is terse; we each tell the other only what we see in front of us. The AC monitors the aircraft response to the terrain depicted on his TF radar presentation. This, combined with the larger picture of the terrain that the WSO is describing to him from his attack-radar presentation, indicates a properly-functioning system. Safe TF-ing requires excellent crew co-ordination, which means practice and trust. Complacency towards TF-ing is unwise and could be fatal. We may argue about the percentage lethality of Triple-A or SAMs, but we all know the ground rates 100 per cent.'

Admittedly, something drastic would have to happen for the TFR to fail completely; the system is dual-channel, and if the operating system should fail the standby system automatically takes over. The descent to terrain-following from high-level cruise is fully automatic and hands-off; once TFR is selected the F-111 loses height at about 10,000 ft per minute until its radar altimeter identifies the ground at 5,000 ft and the levelling-out process is begun. There is no movement of the control column as the aircraft sweeps through valleys and over mountain peaks; the climb and dive commands are fed directly from the TFR computer to the pitch channel of the flight control system.

In Vietnam, the F-111s operated singly and achieved impressive results in their 'blind' first-pass attacks on pinpoint targets, which often lay in the middle of densely populated areas. Crews were instructed that if they could not positively identify these targets and bomb them accurately, they were to bring their bombs home. In the last few months of the war the F-111s flew about 98 per cent of their sorties at low level, on TFR, and on almost every occasion succeeded in dropping twelve or sixteen 'iron' bombs or cluster bombs right on the target's nose. It was an achievement unparalleled in the history of air warfare.

Even though any malfunction of the TFR would automatically initiate a 3 g pull-up to a safe altitude, F-111 crews in Vietnam found the knowledge that the ground was only a fraction of a second beneath them to be far more worrying than enemy action. Salvoes of SAMs and AAA burst were things you could see; the terrain over which you were speeding in darkness and cloud was something you could not, except on radar. As one F-111 pilot put it in an interview with US Air Force Magazine: 'It takes real discipline to come up over these mountains, as we did at night, out on top of the cloud layer in the moonlight. We'd see those jagged peaks all round us poking through the cloud tops, and we'd have to put the nose down back into that mist. And as we went down the moonlight would fade, and the cloud get darker, and we'd know we were descending far below those peaks and were depending on our radars and our autopilots — and with Hanoi coming up, I won't say that I wasn't worried.

'One night, when the weather was *very* bad, I was in cloud for the last eleven minutes before bombs away. That means at the lowest levels of the whole flight, at 250 or 200 ft going up and down the hills, we didn't see a thing outside the cockpit, not even after the bombs left us. For me, this thing was really remarkable. Even now I can't explain how fantastic it was... the confidence I gained in the airplane, it made a believer out of me. Given a choice on a night strike of going in Hi or going in Lo, I'll take Lo every time. And I'll go anywhere in the F-111.'

So would most crews of the 'Aardvark', as the One-Eleven is known unofficially. And there is still a lot of development potential in the aircraft, enough to carry it through the 1990s in its interdictor role; indeed, taking its projected lifespan into account, together with its unique range/payload capability, it may turn out to be irreplaceable. Even the introduction of the F-15E will leave thirty per cent of central European targets within range of only the F-111, and within the Middle East potential target structure that figure rises to seventy per cent. In the emerging role of sea lane monitoring, the F-111 offers a 350 per cent increase in sea coverage over the planned 1990 non-F-111 fighter force.

The F-111 has already shown itself to be adaptable to advanced weapon-delivery systems. Between September 1977 and August 1978, the aircraft's compatability was tested with Pave Tack, a self-contained target acquisition and weapon aiming pod containing forward-looking infra-red for target acquisition and recognition by day and night, and a laser-designator/rangefinder for use with guided weapons such as the Maverick missile and GBU-15 glide bomb.

Tests with the latter weapon included four launches and four direct hits; three bombs passed through a target vehicle and the fourth, released at 1.4M at 22,000 ft, sank a target vessel. Trials with the AGM-65A Maverick TV-guided missile included three launches, two of which resulted in direct hits; in the third instance lock was broken because of a technical fault in the missile guidance system. In other Pave Tack tests, level, dive and toss deliveries of GBU-10 and GBU-16 laser-guided bombs resulted in practically 100 per cent direct hits, and tests with unguided iron bombs showed delivery accuracies roughly twice those attainable with radar. Maximum-range toss deliveries were two-and-a-half times more accurate, while attacks on targets at unknown elevations proved to be as accurate as bombing runs against targets at known altitudes above ground level.

Since 1982, Pave Tack has equipped the F-111Fs of the 48th Tactical Fighter Wing at Lakenheath, in Suffolk. The 1,300 lb pod is stowed in a special weapons bay cradle and is completely recessed inside the bay when not in use, rotating through 180° in five seconds to expose the gimballed sensor head when the system is activated. Once exposed, the sensor head can be rotated to cover the complete lower hemisphere, and provides a stabilized platform for the FLIR, laser ranger and laser designator. The stabilized infra-red image, annotated with range information and a reticle representing the laser designator, is presented on a virtual-image display which replaces the WSO's radar plan position indicator.

The new display comprises two cathode ray tubes, viewed through a magnifying lens, the primary — and larger — display situated above the secondary CRT. The WSO can call up FLIR, radar and weapon imagery on either display; side and centrally-mounted consoles house the necessary switchery for Pave Tack and its associated weapons.

On a low-level run-in to a target, the primary display shows a radar ground map which permits major course corrections to be made. Pave Tack is activated at just under four miles from the target to provide more accurate steering information, and the FLIR image appears on the lower CRT. If he so wishes, the WSO can switch the FLIR imagery to the upper CRT, allowing radar or weapon-seeking images to be presented on the lower display. After selecting the correct FLIR field of view, the operator slews the reticle on to the target and fires the laser, which is kept on target by the aircraft's inertial navigation system even when the F-111 is manoeuvring. The WSO has a hand controller for fine tuning of the laser line of sight. With the laser illuminating the target the F-111's central computer initiates a 3 g pull-up to weapon release point; as the aircraft turns away from the target Pave Tack's sensor head rotates so that it continues to provide illumination until bomb impact. The pod is then retracted and the aircraft accelerates to supersonic speed for its escape from the target area.

Chapter 8
The F-4 Phantom: NATO's workhorse warplane

On 27 May 1958, McDonnell's chief test pilot took a new combat aircraft into the air from Lambert Field, St Louis, on a twenty-minute maiden flight. That aircraft was the F4H-1 Phantom II. Nearly thirty years later, its designation having in the meantime changed to F-4, the Phantom is still one of the world's most significant combat aircraft.

For the US Navy crews who were the first to fly it operationally, the Phantom represented an enormous technological leap forward; yet few of them could have dreamed how advances in avionics and weaponry would enhance the aircraft's potency over the next quarter-century. Pilots and RIOs (Radar Intercept Officers) were enthusiastic about the way the Phantom and its systems handled right from the beginning, a view that is admirably reflected in this description by Commander William A. Mackay, USN, of what it was like to fly an F-4B while he was a production test pilot with the McDonnell Aircraft Corporation in the early 1960s. The basics remain the same, but when one considers the kit that modern Phantom crews have to handle, it all sounds simple.

'Since every production version is capable of attaining near-record altitudes on every flight, the pilot will want to be prepared and wear a pressure suit. In fact, wearing the suit on every flight is an excellent way for the pilot to become fully acquainted with it. In a very few hours he will be feeling completely at home. The pressure suit used with the Phantom is the Navy's Mk IV Md 1 Lightweight Full Pressure Suit made by the B.F. Goodrich Company. It is both comfortable and mobile, and will become immediately pressurized if the cabin pressurization drops below psia. It offers protection against rapid decompression, wind blast and cold, and from the hazards of extreme altitudes. It is automatic and operates under all conditions, including ejection.

'For the period while pilot and RIO are being transported to the airplane from the ready-room they carry small, light portable air conditioning units that afford ventilation air to their suits.

'Despite the plane's complexity and density, walk-around inspection of the F-4B can be accomplished in a few minutes and is as simple and routine as the inspection of any modern jet interceptor. I usually have my RIO accompany me on this brief tour and follow recommended procedures set forth in the pilot's handbook, checking for fuel or hydraulic leaks, removal of protective covers, and proper pressure gauge readings.

'External canopy operation is accomplished pneumatically by depressing individual buttons on the left exterior of the fuselage just below each canopy. Normal access to the cockpit is made via a built-in boarding ladder and two kick-in steps located on the left side of the forward fuselage. This convenient feature eliminates the necessity of a separate ladder which is always a hazard during carrier operations where high winds across the deck are routine and a loose object blowing down the flight deck could result in injury to personnel.

'Naturally, this up-to-date fighter is equipped with the latest in ejection seats, the Martin Baker, which provides both low level and high altitude escape capability. Strapping into the seat is accomplished easily and rapidly by use of a pilot's integrated flight harness designed for use with the seat.

'The pilot's right console contains an orderly arrangement of the communication and navigation control switches, external and internal light controls, wing folding control, generator switches, and cabin temperature and pressurization controls. The left console contains the throttles, fuel control panel, AFCS (Automatic Flight Control System) panel, engine control panels, emergency handles for canopy, flaps and hydraulic/generators, and drag chute handle.

'The right vertical panel contains a grouping of all warning lights. When a malfunction occurs, a master caution light illuminates on the main instrument panel simultaneously with the relevant one on the warning light panel. This reduces the amount of instrument surveillance required by the pilot since he need only watch the Master Caution light for an indication of trouble and then refer to the warning light panel for a definition of his problem. The left vertical panel provides indication of wheel and flap position and trim settings.

'The main instrument panel is designed for maximum ease of

When US Navy pilots first became acquainted with the F-4 Phantom, they converted from types such as the McDonnell F 3H Demon and the North American FJ-4 Fury, which were essentially stop-gap aircraft. The Phantom represented a great leap forward in the air superiority game.

scanning under instrument conditions. The Attitude Director Indicator (ADI) is a very imposing 5-in diameter instrument located in the centre of the panel. It provides attitude and heading information in all three axes simultaneously with flight director indication. Directly below it is the Horizontal Situation Indicator (HSI) which is the same size and provides the horizontal or plan view of the aircraft with respect to the navigation situation. Forming a T arrangement with the two instruments described above are the Airspeed and Mach number indicator on the left of the ADI and the counter pointer type altimeter on the right.

'The aircraft's impingement starting system eliminates the need for the usual bulky, heavy starters found in most airplanes. Air from an external source is distributed to the left or right engine, depending on the pilot's selection. The actual start procedure is very simple and straightforward. After the external air and electrical power sources are connected, the pilot turns on the engine master, then the starter switch, waits until the engine reaches 10–11 per cent and then depresses the ignition button on the appropriate throttle and moves the throttle to idle position. The throttles are standard, going forward and inboard from OFF to IDLE and then forward to the stop for full military power. For afterburner the throttle is moved outboard and forward from full military.

'For taxi-ing and ground control, the Phantom is provided with nosewheel steering (or if the pilot so desires he can steer the aircraft by differential braking of the main wheels). To engage the steering control, the pilot simply presses a button on the control stick and then guides the airplane directionally with the rudder pedals. Once the plane is rolling, idle power is usually adequate to keep it rolling at the proper taxi speed. Taxi-ing the Phantom is when the pilot first begins to feel that this is the airplane for him. There is none of the "shake, rattle and roll" associated with some of the other jets I have flown. The machine moves along smoothly and with a very solid feel.

'Checking of the engines prior to take-off must be done individually since running them up simultaneously above 85 per cent rpm could result in skidding or tyre rotation on the wheels. Although full flap take-offs are acceptable for normal field use, half-flaps are preferred since there is a reduction in drag, increased power (less bleed air being used for Boundary Layer Control), only a small loss of lateral control, increased stabilator effectiveness, best configuration for single engine, and less trim change while cleaning up. No-flap field take-offs are permissible if the situation warrants it. Full flap take-offs are necessary for shipboard catapult launches.

'My procedure for taking off in the F-4B is as follows. After the engines have been checked individually and the airplane lined up on the runway with take-off clearance received from the tower, I advance throttles to about 80 per cent and release brakes. Power is then advanced to full military and a rapid check of engine instruments is made prior to moving into afterburner. After the afterburners are lighted another check is made of the engine gauges, especially the EGT (Exhaust Gas Temperature) and nozzle position indicators. The rudder becomes effective for directional control at about 80 kt and the nose strut can be extended at about 110–115 kt with light back pressure on the stick. This enables the use of only moderate back stick to lift off at about 145 kt. A good rule-of-thumb trim setting for any take-off flap configuration is neutral for rudder, stabilator and ailerons.

'In my brief description of the take-off, I note that I failed to emphasize sufficiently the phenomenal acceleration of the F-4B when using A/B [afterburn]. It is so rapid that, even if he is prepared for it, the first couple of take-offs will find the Phantom pilot having a difficult time absorbing much of what happened and asking himself how he got to 40,000 ft when he wanted to stop at

What air superiority is all about: a USAF Phantom intercepts a Soviet Tu-95 ELINT aircraft off Alaska.

30,000. So to make sure that on the first few rides pilot and Phantom know who's flying whom, I recommend only full military power be used for take-offs.

'When the airplane is positively airborne, raise the landing gear. Since even a clean take-off can be made at 160 kt, flaps can be started up at this speed which will be easily attained by the time the pilot has put the gear handle in "up" position. Immediately after getting airborne with gear and flaps retracting, there will be a noticeable nose-up tendency which is readily controllable and easily trimmed out. In A/B quite a nose-up attitude is required to hold down acceleration enough for gear and flaps to clean up prior to reaching limit speeds.

'On reaching an altitude of 35 to 40,000 ft the pilot will find the airplane handles very well in subsonic flight regimes. Three axis dampers are available and he will feel quite comfortable orbiting and conserving fuel while awaiting assignment of an intercept mission. Longitudinally, in the area of transonic flight, the machine becomes even more stable in both static and manoeuvring stability. Lateral control system and rudder remain effective in this range with little noticeable change. Overall, the plane remains highly manoeuvrable in the transonic speed range. In the supersonic region stabilator effectiveness is reduced as Mach number increases; however, the airplane still manoeuvres quite well out to

High over the North Sea, a Victor tanker of No 55 Squadron refuels a Phantom FGR 2 of No 29 Squadron.

0.2M+ speeds. Roll rate and response is reduced at high supersonic speeds, but remains sufficiently high to permit rapid manoeuvring at all speeds. The rudder remains effective but is reduced considerably in yawing power at high Mach numbers. Longitudinal damping is highly positive at all supersonic speeds.

'The Phantom provides the pilot with a very fine AFCS which is an electro-hydraulic autopilot capable of performing two modes of operation, damper and autopilot. The damper improves stability in pitch, roll and yaw and can be used while the plane is being flown manually. The autopilot mode maintains any heading and/or attitude selected by the pilot within autopilot limits. It is also capable of holding any altitude or Mach number selected. For a change in heading or attitude, movement of the normal flight control stick will effect the change without the necessity of disengagement and re-engagement of the autopilot. Normal disengagement is simply the reverse of the engagement sequence, but an emergency or rapid disconnect feature is provided on the control stick which disengages the entire autopilot.

'Despite the Phantom's amazing take-off performance the pilot is in for an even more pleasant surprise when he receives an order to abandon his subsonic orbit station and intercept an inbound target as soon as possible. The time required to accelerate from about 0.85M to a speed in excess of 2.0M is truly remarkable and in my opinion places the Phantom foremost among the world's fighters.

'Hydraulically operated speed brakes, mounted on the underside of the inboard wing panels, are very effective in slowing the aircraft and can be extended at any speed. Pitch trim change required during extension is surprisingly small.

'The final phases to be discussed are slow flight and landing, and here the Phantom gives the Navy pilot final proof that it meets the full requirements of an outstanding carrier-based interceptor. The pilot is provided with angle-of-attack indexers which are installed on each side of the windshield. The indexers present angle-of-attack information during a landing approach by illuminating symbolic cutouts. They are located so as to be readily seen at all times during a carrier or field landing. This permits the pilot to devote more of his attention to line-up and rate of descent.

'For an airplane which has better than a twelve-to-one ratio of top speed to landing approach speed, it is probably surprising to read that the Phantom is completely free of any unusual or tricky

In this photograph, which shows the value of expert camouflage, an RF-4C Phantom of the 10th Tactical Reconnaissance Wing, USAFE (Alconbury) flies low over the Scottish landscape.

landing characteristics. In fact, it is probably more comfortable to the pilot, mentally, because of the abundance of power available for wave-off or recovery from a sagging approach.

'Entry to the break for a normal landing can be made at any airspeed dictated by the local course rules. Speed brake extension and a tight turn will always reduce speed to the landing gear maximum by the time the 180° position is reached. For my own standardization purposes I usually hit the brake at about 350 kt. Extending the landing gear and flaps produces a negligible attitude and trim change. The noise and buffet that comes out of the nosewheel gear-well during gear extension smooths out and disappears as approach speeds are reached.

'Full flaps are used for normal landings, but half flaps are recommended for single engine approaches for obvious reasons. At about the 180° position I recheck the gear and flap indicators for a down indication and retract speed brakes to decrease buffet. Here I also usually check the Aileron Rudder Interconnect (ARI) system. This is a special system that the Phantom has which causes rudder displacement porportional to aileron displacement and provides co-ordinated turns at low airspeeds. The limits of the system are 15° of rudder displacement when the damper is engaged and 10° rudder when the damper switch is OFF.

'As I roll into the base leg with a moderate rate of descent, I continue to reduce speed so that about the time I hit the 90° position I am about 10–15 kt above final approach speed. I am paying very close attention to the approach indexer to ensure that I don't get slower than "on-speed" indication. When on final approach (I try to plan the base leg to allow for about a one mile straightaway final), I attempt to establish a 700 ft-a-minute descent aiming for a touchdown point within the first 1,000 ft of runway. I do not attempt to flare or chop power prior to crossing the end of the runway, because when making a power approach in this bird, deceleration with throttles retarded is rapid due to power response and it is going to start settling very fast. Immediately after touchdown I retard throttles to idle, deploy drag chute and hold the nosewheel off as long as possible to take advantage of aerodynamic braking. The nosewheel will fall through to the runway after the plane has slowed only 20–25 kt.

'Crosswind characteristics are good and no special techniques are necessary to accomplish the approach and touchdown, except that no effort should be made to hold the nosewheel off after landing. The pilot should also feel free to engage nose gear steering at any time after touchdown to assist in directional control.

'Single-engined landings can be considered basically the same as a normal landing. The single-engine flight characteristics are essentially the same as normal flight characteristics due to the proximity of thrust lines to centre of the airplane. Slight rudder deflection is required to prevent yaw towards the failed engine. The aircraft design is such that no one safety of flight requirement is dependent on a specific engine. Thus, loss of an engine will not

Like the F-4 Phantom, the F-100 Super Sabre was a 1950s' aircraft designed to intercept high-flying bombers. Unlike the Phantom, it did not prove so readily adaptable to close support work in Vietnam.

affect safe aircraft operation. As mentioned before, wing flap position would be one half in this case. If the necessity for a single-engine wave-off should occur, the Phantom will have the situation well under control. It has ample thrust to accomplish the wave-off snappily without having to resort to afterburner. The afterburner is available, however, and should be used when the pilot so desires.'

Phantoms flew their first combat mission over South Vietnam on 13 April 1965, when twelve F-4Bs of Marine Fighter/Attack Squadron VMFA-531, normally based at Atsugi in Japan, operated out of Da Nang in support of US Marine ground troops. The ground-attack sortie was led by Lieutenant Colonel William C. McGraw Jr., the unit's commanding officer. During subsequent operations the Phantom proved highly successful in the ground support role, carrying an average warload of 5,000 lb. In October 1966 RF-4B Phantoms also began to replace RF-8A Crusaders in Marine Corps recce squadron VMCJ-1, providing a round-the-clock intelligence-gathering capability. As time went by, night infra-red reconnaissance played a growing part in the overall effort.

In November 1965, the Phantom strength in Vietnam was boosted with the arrival at Bien Hoa and Da Nang of the 12th Tactical Fighter Wing, with F-4Cs. These aircraft were initially used in combat air patrol (CAP) role and were committed to ground support operations gradually, employing tactics developed by the Marine Corps earlier in the year. F-4Cs had already been operating over North Vietnam on a smaller scale for several months, and on 23 July 1965 the first was shot down by an SA-2 SAM; prior to this, on 10 July, the Phantom had scored its first air-to-air kills when two MiG-17s were shot down by a pair of F-4Cs (Captains Thomas S. Roberts and Ronald C. Anderson in one and Captains Kenneth E. Holcombe and Arthur C. Clark in the other).

In September 1966, with the USAF's 'Rolling Thunder' air strike operations against North Vietnam in full swing, the North Vietnamese Air Force suddenly began to fight back in strength, and the USAF's F-4Cs were temporarily diverted from their primary strike mission to air combat against the MiGs. The latter were mainly MiG-21s, armed with Atoll infra-red homing missiles and operating from five bases in the Hanoi area; at this stage of the war, American pilots were restricted from attacking objectives close to the North Vietnamese capital.

Over Vietnam, Phantoms mainly operated in conjunction with Lockheed EC-121 surveillance aircraft, which vectored them towards likely targets and warned of the approach of enemy aircraft.

The tactics employed by the MiG pilots involved flying low and then zooming up to attack the heavily-laden fighter-bombers — mainly F-105 Thunderchiefs — forcing them to jettison their bomb loads as a matter of survival. To counter this, Phantoms armed with Sidewinder AAMs flew at lower altitudes than the Thunderchiefs, enabling the crews to spot the MiGs at an early stage in their interception attempt and then use the Phantom's superior speed and acceleration to engage the enemy. These were very much in the nature of hit-and-run tactics, the Phantom pilots avoiding turning combat because of the MiG-21's superior manoeuvrability, but they worked; the Phantom crews had a superb early warning facility in the shape of EC-121 aircraft, which were able to direct the CAP fighters on to their targets in good time. In 1966, American fighters destroyed 23 MiGs for the loss of nine of their own aircraft.

Early in 1967, 'Rolling Thunder' operations were expanded to include targets in the Hanoi area, which were defended by about a hundred MiGs. To inflict the maximum destruction on the latter the Americans planned a ruse code-named Operation Bolo, which was designed to bring the MiGs to battle. Thunderchief strike aircraft were used as bait, and they were supported by 56 Phantoms of the 8th and 366th Tactical Fighter Wings as well as 24 defence-suppression F-105s and EB-66 electronic warfare aircraft for radar jamming.

The 8th TFW's Phantoms were led by Colonel Robin Olds, a highly experienced fighter leader with eight victories to his credit during the Second World War. In the air battle that took place on that day, 2 January 1967, he and his Phantom pilots destroyed seven MiGs in twelve minutes for no loss, Olds himself accounting for one of them. The action is ably described by Mike Spick in his book *Fighter Pilot Tactics* (Patrick Stephens Ltd, 1983).

'The first [MiG] appeared directly astern and Olds broke left, turning just hard enough to spoil the MiG's aim, and waited for his Nos 3 and 4 to clear his tail. As he did so, another MiG appeared just off to the left at about 1½ miles range. Olds let fly with a brace of Sparrows but they failed to reach their targets. The Sparrow was notoriously unreliable unless fired under ideal conditions and battle conditions are rarely ideal. The initial range of about a mile-and-a-half was probably reduced to less than a mile by the time the radar had been locked on and the missile fired. Against a manoeuvring target this distance was too short for the Sparrow's tracking capability to cope. The MiG-21 disappeared into the clouds, but another emerged off to Colonel Olds' left, in a hard turn towards him. Olds pulled the nose of his Phantom up at about 45° and rolled to the right. Half inverted, he waited as the MiG passed beneath, then rolled down astern to a position about 20° angle off and just under a mile range. He launched two Sidewinders, one of which hit and blew the MiG's right wing off.'

Two more MiGs were shot down by Phantoms on 6th January, and following these losses there was a marked decrease in North Vietnamese air activity. The next major engagements took place in April and May, when USAF crews, mostly in Phantoms, destroyed twenty MiGs in fifty separate air combats.

Phantoms of the US Navy's Task Force 77 were involved over Vietnam from 4 August 1964, when aircraft from the USS *Constellation* struck enemy PT boat bases at Loc Chao. The US Navy's first MiG kills were scored in June 1967, the first on the 17th when F-4s from the USS *Midway's* VF-21, flown by Commander Louis C. Page and Lieutenant John C. Smith (RIO) and Lieutenant Jack E.D. Batson shot down to MiGs fifty miles south of Hanoi. The action began at 10:26 when Commander Page, heading north-east, established radar contact with bogies several miles ahead. The two Phantoms and four MiGs approached each other head-on at a closing speed of 1,000 kt — in other words a mile every three-and-a-half seconds — and Commander Page made visual contact with the enemy, identifying them as MiG-17s. He fired a Sparrow at the second of the four MiGs, which were flying in ragged line astern, and Lieutenant Batson launched a Sparrow at the third. On this occasion there was no problem with the AAMs and both MiGs went down in flames.

The Navy's Phantoms proved their worth in the flak suppression role during 'Rolling Thunder'. On one occasion, on 29 June 1966, flak suppression F-4s of the USS *Ranger's* VF-142, led by Commander Jim Brown, attacked flak sites in support of Skyhawk strikes against oil targets in the Haiphong area and placed their bombs so accurately that it seemed as though the heavy-calibre AAA had been turned off by the flick of a switch. In the same operation, Phantoms of VF-143 positioned their aircraft between the MiG bases and the strike aircraft, preventing enemy fighters from breaking through.

The Vietnam War showed that the Phantom, although a superlative strike aircraft, was a long way from being a fighter in the strict sense of the word. It was not designed as such. The F-4's built-in interception role was designed to enable it to shoot down enemy bombers at long range with its missile armament; in turning combat it was no match for nimble aircraft like the MiG-21.

Operations over Vietnam also led to some Phantom airframe redesign. At low airspeeds, or during combat manoeuvres at high weights, the F-4 had a serious stall problem that had already resulted in the loss of several aircraft before the type was ever deployed in Vietnam. Another problem was the aircraft's high sink rate. Both these shortcomings were spotlighted by two recorded accidents suffered by the USAF's Phantom force during training in the United States.

In the first of these, the pilot of an F-4C was practising a series of air combat manoeuvres following some practice interceptions. Several turns were made while descending to 15,000 ft. The pilot reported that the aircraft entered a 'burble' condition at about 180 kt. He relaxed back pressure on the stick and the airspeed increased. At 260 kt he again attempted back pressure on the stick, but the aircraft failed to respond. Afterburner was selected with no

The RF-4C Phantom still performs a vital reconnaissance role. Pictured is an aircraft of the 1st Tactical Reconnaissance Squadron, 10th Tactical Reconnaissance Wing, Alconbury.

improvement and the aircraft entered a nose low spiral. The pilot deployed the drag chute in an attempt to recover from a post-stall gyration, but the aircraft continued descending rapidly in a nose low spiral, which was unresponsive to control movement. The crew ejected successfully at 6,000 ft. The prime cause of the accident was pilot error, with insufficient height to recover from a post-stall dive and spiral.

In the second accident, the crew of an F-4C was on its first practice nuclear mission. The aircraft was observed in the pull-up for an over-the-shoulder delivery, but when next sighted the aircraft was seen in a gliding descent near one of the range towers. As the aircraft neared the ground, full power was applied but the sink rate could not be checked. The pilot tried to eject, but was too late. The primary cause of the accident was given as the failure of the pilot to apply power soon enough to recover from a low airspeed, high sink rate position.

Problems such as these caused growing concern in Vietnam, where Phantoms were called upon to operate at high gross weight and to perform violent manoeuvres at low altitude. Accidental losses began to reach alarming proportions, and as a result the USAF asked McDonnell to redesign the wing leading edge, the blown flaps being replaced by powerful maneouvring slats that extended automatically at high angles of attack. These devices, which claimed to improve the lift by 33 per cent, were incorporated on aircraft on the F-4E production line and subsequently retrofitted to all USAF Phantoms, as well as many destined for export.

Inescapably, the Phantom is a weapon system designed with the technology of the 1950s, to perform certain functions in keeping with the operational requirements of that decade — the most important of which was to provide an effective defence against the high-speed, high-altitude nuclear-armed bomber. Over Vietnam, performing different roles, it came into conflict with the technology of the 1960s — SAMs and radar-controlled AAA — and its shortcomings became apparent. They became even more apparent in October 1973, during the Yom Kippur War, when the Israeli Air Force operated F-4E Phantoms in hostile airspace where — for the first time in its history — it lacked total air superiority.

The IAF's Phantoms first went into action in September 1969 in a series of air strikes against Egyptian artillery positions on the West Bank of the Suez Canal. The strike squadrons then set about the systematic destruction of Egyptian missile and radar sites in the

Canal Zone, concentrating on installations spread along an eighteen-mile-wide defence perimeter between the Canal and Cairo, and on strategic roads in the same area. In two months, the strike aircraft — Phantoms and Skyhawks — destroyed twelve SA-2 SAM sites and some twenty early warning radar stations.

On 7 January 1970, IAF Phantoms — profiting from the serious disruption to the Egyptian missile and radar defences — attacked targets in the vicinity of Cairo. It was the beginning of an intensive period of air strikes against targets in the heart of Egypt, using both Phantoms and Mirages. On 3 February, six Mirages and two Phantoms attacked the big Egyptian Air Force supply base at El Khanka, thirteen miles north-west of Cairo, with rockets, napalm and delayed-action bombs, causing severe damage. The bomb load of one of the Phantoms, however, became hung-up for a fraction of a second because of an electrical fault and went down on a metal works at Abu Zabal, about a mile north of the target area, killing seventy civilians and injuring 98 others.

In just over a month, the Phantoms and Mirages made a total of nine deep-penetration raids into Egypt, attacking military depots near Cairo. The IAF's orders were clear; the Egyptians, whose commandos were carrying out an increasing number of attacks on the Israeli-held east bank of the Canal, were to be allowed no respite that would enable them to move large quantities of war material up to the Canal Zone in preparation for a large-scale raid into Sinai. The pressure was maintained, but only at a price; from 7 January to 7 February 1970 the IAF lost nine aircraft, including one Phantom.

The spring of 1970 saw the Phantoms engaged in attacks on Egyptian SA-3 missile sites which had recently been springing up along the Canal Zone and which presented a far greater threat to the attackers than the SA-2, for the SA-3 was specifically designed to engage fast, low-flying aircraft. In May, Phantoms visited Ras Banas to attack Egyptian shipping as a reprisal for the sinking of an Israeli fishing vessel and an attack on Eilat harbour by Egyptian Navy frogmen. The raid involved a round flight of 1,300 miles, and was intended partly as an indication to the Egyptians that — in spite of their new SA-3s — the IAF was still capable of striking at any spot on Egyptian territory. Attacking through heavy anti-aircraft fire, the Phantoms sank a 2,575-ton Z-Class destroyer and a Soviet-built Komar-class missile boat, the latter with 20 mm M61A1 gunfire.

The Yom Kippur War, which began on 6 October 1973 with an

Royal Navy and Royal Air Force Phantoms display their distinctive profiles at air shows during the late 1960s. The RAF aircraft, seen tucking up its undercarriage, bears the markings of No 43 Squadron.

armoured attack on two fronts — by 70,000 Egyptian troops supported by 400 tanks across the Suez Canal, and by Syrian forces in the Golan Heights — was the sternest test the IAF had so far had to face, because the Arab armies were supported by an enormous concentration of anti-aircraft weaponry. As well as the SA-2s and SA-3s, mobile SA-6 SAM systems and ZSU-23/4 tracked AAA systems, each with four radar-controlled 23 mm guns, were brought into play. The IAF's Phantom force was used primarily in the missile suppression role and suffered heavy losses, mainly because the relatively flat terrain offered no protection while carrying out low-level attacks. Israeli pilots adopted new tactics which involved diving their aircraft steeply on the SAM sites, which kept their aircraft outside the low-angle missile launch trajectory; unfortunately this brought them within range of the AAA, which in fact accounted for the majority of the Israeli losses.

The Yom Kippur War showed that, in an environment dominated by modern SAM and AAA systems, the Phantom was a far from ideal ground attack aircraft unless it was provided with a stand-off attack capability. Other air forces had been quick to realise these limitations; the Royal Air Force re-equipped its ground attack squadrons with the Jaguar and Harrier, leaving the Phantom to the air defence role — a task that it still performs admirably, because it is the one for which it was originally intended. In Luftwaffe service, too, the Phantom has only a secondary ground-attack role, being biased towards air combat. In the air-to-air role, the Luftwaffe's F-4Fs carry out classic airborne interceptions; the pilot guided to visual contact point by his RIO's radar. The radar target display appears in the pilot's gunsight in the form of a target symbol which the pilot flies into coincidence with an aiming symbol, the target aircraft's attitude and closing speed being displayed at the same time. Once the target is locked on, the pilot can fly an interception using the gunsight alone, and would normally launch a Sidewinder. For M61 cannon attacks, the sight reverts to a normal gyro lead-computing mode and the gun is harmonized for an optimum range of 2,000 ft. The normal air-to-ground firing range is 2,800 ft with the aircraft flying at between 450 and 550 kt.

In the air-to-air role the Luftwaffe's Phantom crews practice a great deal of visual interception, working on the principle that in wartime the GCI stations would be heavily blanketed by enemy ECM. The usual technique involves a pair of Phantoms flying CAP over the battle area, with one aircraft at about 10,000 ft and the second a mile away, flying between 3,000 ft and 6,000 ft higher or lower. If a four-ship formation is used, the lead pair would fly in line abreast with a mile separation, and the trailing pair would be lower down and astern.

In the air-to-ground role the Phantoms operate in pairs, flying at about 800 ft, using their radar for navigation. The aircraft are equipped with the ALN-10 radar homing and warning system and the APR-36V threat display to give warning of enemy CAP. Close to the target area the aircraft descend to 250 ft and make their pass over the target at about 550 kt. Retarded and cluster bombs are the most usual weapons employed, and Phantom crews have developed a skip-bombing technique whereby the bombs are released at 200 ft in level flight and then bounce, reaching a height of 30 ft and a forward distance of 100 ft before exploding. A considerable degree of accuracy has been attained with this method, which is useful against targets such as individual buildings.

Luftwaffe Phantom crews used to practice dive-bombing techniques against small targets, but these were abandoned after the bitter lessons learned by the Israeli Air Force in 1973 became known. It takes only six seconds for a Soviet SAM system to lock on, which makes a diving aircraft extremely vulnerable.

Despite its age, the Phantom remains a viable weapons system; in 1985 it was operated by ten nations, including the United States, with about 850 aircraft in service worldwide. And maybe the story of the F-4 does not end here, for at the time of writing the Boeing Company is proposing a 'Super Phantom', re-engined with the Pratt & Whitney PW1120 turbojet developing 20,000 lb/st and a full avionics upgrade comprising a multi-mode radar, head-up and head-down cockpit displays and a laser-gyro inertial navigation system.

The modernization would certainly give a massive boost to the old warhorse's performance. Boeing estimates that a Super Phantom with three external tanks would require a take-off roll of 2,600 ft compared with 3,300 ft for the standard F-4, and that its acceleration from 0.6M to 1.2M would improve by 27 per cent for a clean aircraft with 50 per cent internal fuel remaining. Sustained turn rate at 0.9M and 15,000 ft would improve too, from 9° per second to 10.5° per second.

Avionics being studied for the potential Super Phantom include the Westinghouse APG-66 radar, Marconi HUD, Sperry cockpit display and the Honeywell laser INS. This, together with enhanced manoeuvrability and an advanced medium-range AAM armament, would enable the Super Phantom to engage low-flying aircraft adequately for several years to come.

If, as has been suggested, the entire Gross National Product of the United States will not be sufficient, by the end of the next century, to buy a single example of a new fighter aircraft if the present upward spiral of development costs continues, it may be that the development of existing airframes to the limit will be the only logical course. It is strange to think that the Phantom, the ultimate fighter of its day, may still be operating alongside the ultimate fighter of the 21st century.

Chapter 9
Flight into the future

As these words are being written, the pattern of military aviation for the 21st century is being set by futuristic combat aircraft projects which are now on the drawing-boards of the world's leading aircraft designers. Some of these designs are natural progressions; Mach Two V/STOL fighters, for example, or air superiority fighters with avionics so advanced that they will control the aircraft's entire behaviour in tight-turning air combat, leaving the pilot with little to do except monitor his systems.

Such aircraft will fly and fight from ground level up to the stratosphere: but what about the realms beyond? As a natural consequence of superpower politics, military aviation is slowly and inexorably moving into a space environment. F-15 Eagles, armed with ASAT and zoom-climbing to extreme altitudes, already have the capability to shoot down satellites, while the Space Shuttle can launch and retrieve military payloads. Other, smaller shuttle-type craft now being designed in both east and west could be the prototypes of craft that will one day be able to take off under their own power with conventional turbojets, then switch to rocket power for manoeuvring in close earth orbit.

To get an idea of what it might be like to fly what we had better call a 'space fighter', we need to go a short distance back in time — to the 1960s, in fact, and the North American X-15. The Space Shuttle is a cargo ship, so the X-15 is the nearest thing that has yet flown to the type of craft that might be flying CAP in earth orbit sometime in the future. And who better to describe what the X-15 was like to fly than Colonel Bob White, who in 1962 took it to a height of 59.6 miles and became the first pilot to qualify for the US Astronaut's wings in a fixed-wing aircraft.

'...The cockpit of the aeroplane was not really a radical departure from the cockpit any pilot is used to looking at. The presentations had certain unique items associated with them to provide us with information we were looking for, because of the flight regime we were operating in. We had a number of unusual things, however; we had three control sticks in the aeroplane at the beginning of the programme. Aerodynamic control was provided through the centre stick and a side stick. We felt that this side stick was necessary because of the high acceleration the pilot would experience during the entry manoeuvre to the atmosphere, particularly when he would be subject to over five gs in the normal direction and four gs longitudinally. So it was important there, particularly in the event of control problems. We did not want inadvertent inputs into the control system so the side controller would allow the pilot, we believed, more precise control in the event of that situation.

'For reaction controls we had small rockets in the nose and the wingtips of the aeroplane to control the aeroplane's attitude outside the atmosphere; that was initially provided by a small controller on the left side of the cockpit. The ballistic controls, with that small controller on the left side of the cockpit, allowed the pilot to control a flow of hydrogen peroxide through the lines to the appropriate rocket in the nose and wings. We had a combination of silver and stainless steel screens as the catalyst bed and when the hydrogen peroxide poured over it the chemical reaction resulted in water vapour. Consequently there was steam, but by exhausting it through the appropriate rocket motor we were able to develop thrust and control the aeroplane.

'At the beginning of the programme there was discussion and debate on what kind of escape system we should have. A great deal of talk centred around an entire capsule system. This was used in an earlier vehicle, the X-2 aeroplane, and looking at the problem closely we decided that the capsule would not be ready, fully tested and acceptable for the aeroplane until long after the aeroplane would be ready for flight. The combination of the ejection seat and pressure suit provided, we felt, an adequate system for escape if necessary; the pressure suit that the pilot wears was an integral part of the escape system in that it provided blast and heat protection for the pilot. We had telescoping booms subsequently applied to the seat and big folding arms that flipped out to provide stability. The system was good from 80 kt at ground level to 4.0M at 120,000 ft. We did not plan for escape at the higher altitudes because by the time we arrived all our fuel was expended so the fire and explosion hazard was considerably removed, and the limitations imposed at

4.0M and 120,000 ft were necessary because you have the same re-entry problem as the aeroplane, which means a lot of temperature.

Another item was the pressure suit. This was an interesting device, very uncomfortable I might add, although this particular item was certainly a wonderful garment. We had a system in the aeroplane whereby we pressurized the cockpit with nitrogen gas, something I think that would be unacceptable for the future and in any vehicle that you are going to use on a long term basis. Consequently, the pilot could never open up the face mask — it always had to be closed. A seal kept the nitrogen in the suit away from the oxygen in the helmet. It is rather significant, I think, that after wearing this suit for a number of hours with cooling air circulating through, it nevertheless became very hot and when you took the suit off there were a number of welts and scratch marks all over your body!

'The dropping of the X-15 from the B-52 at launch did not come as a complete surprise to the pilot, because the X-15 pilot was the one who initiated this. It could be done either way and early in the programme we let the B-52 pilot count down and drop you off; later on, when the very last stages of engine operation before light-up were extremely critical, the X-15 pilot himself would flip the switch which would allow him to drop away. The departure from the B-52 pylon was rather sudden, yielding about zero g, and there was a sharp roll off to the right, but this was corrected immediately upon leaving the B-52 flow field. The pilot lit the engine and was on his way. If there was a long delay before engine ignition the pilot could glide at an 8° angle of attack which was near the best lift-drag ration for glide, approximately 240 kt in this case; a fully-loaded aeroplane responded very well and was completely free of buffet. If the angle of attack was increased to 10° a very mild buffet onset was immediately detected and this allowed the pilot to make corrections well in advance of any stall condition.

'Very quickly after the engine light-off we obtained supersonic speed; we rotated to a 10° angle of attack and maintained this 10° until we had the climb-out pitch angle that we wanted on a particular flight, which was dictated by the mission requirement. Buffet was completely absent when we got above 1.0M; there was a mild nose-down trim change between 1.1 and 1.4 but we went through this region so rapidly that we did not even notice it. After initial rotation at the 10° angle of attack we maintained a constant pitch angle and this varied anywhere from 30 to near 40°; we established that, maintained it to engine burn-out, and the acceleration just before burn-out reached 4 g along the longitudinal axis.

'This is chest-to-back g force and was quite sufficient to hold you firmly in your seat. You found that your breathing became a little more shallow but it did not in any way impair your ability to manage your tests. I tried to take my head away from the head rest at 4 g and it was impossible. From engine burn-out until the re-entry the aircraft followed a ballistic trajectory and a unique feature here was the weightlessness experienced by the pilot which occurred for about two minutes. Then there was the requirement that the reaction controls be used since the dynamic pressures had decreased to a minimum of 1 lb per square foot at the highest altitude. Then we followed with the re-entry manoeuvre which terminated when the aircraft rotated to level flight. After experiencing from the high end about 5.6 normal g, 4 g back-to-chest, we came level at 70,000 ft and the peak Q, dynamic pressure, was usually in excess of 1600 lb/sq ft.

'Thrust termination produced no transient aircraft motion due to thrust misalignment. Thrust termination was very sharp and it merely alleviated the longitudinal g. After engine burn-out we trimmed the stabilizer to maintain zero angles of attack. This change in trim was usually complete at about 160,000 ft on the way up and the Q, the dynamic pressure, was decreased to less than 26 lb/sq ft by this time.

'We thought the controls were extremely effective and we were developing the accelerations that we wanted in all axes. At first the response in pitch using reaction controls was a little bit more than desired, but as soon as the pilot had a few experiences there was no problem at all.

'The re-entry was the most interesting thing from the pilot's standpoint. Now, during this course of the flight, on the way up after engine burn-out, this was where we were doing our aeroplane upsets and stability tests, but this was not particularly pertinent to the other handling quality opinions. The re-entry was flown at the relatively higher angles of attack; it was necessary to maintain the high angles of attack on re-entry to stay away from the boundary conditions that existed at the lower end. While flying at lower altitudes in the order of 100,000 ft or so, which we did initially, we could elevate the angle of attack, fail dampers, kick the aeroplane about and make determinations on how good or how poor it might be. But in that case, if we started to lose the aeroplane we had a diverging situation coming up. It was easy at that altitude to reduce the angle of attack back into the good flying area and then come down and recover. But again, at very high altitude we had to maintain high angle of attack; on the re-entry we had rapidly changing conditions of dynamic pressure, temperature, velocity, and all the changes of the aircraft stability and responses.

'You actually begin that manoeuvre as the aeroplane passes through about 180,000 ft on the way down. You trim the stabilizer to some value that should maintain re-entry normal g as the dynamic pressure increases. Before that time we used the reaction control to establish the angle of attack that we wanted to maintain on re-entry, and of course used the trim control to get the stabilizer in its proper position to take care of the situation as the dynamic pressure increased. On re-entry we had a side-slip oscillation that developed — it was small in magnitude, just a few degrees, and was quite high in frequency, but since it was low enough in magnitude essentially we disregarded it and never had the dampers fail in this situation.

'I will mention several control features that were common to every flight before I get to the landing phase. The speed brakes were used throughout the speed and altitude range, under thrust and after engine shut-down and, except for incremental use in the landing pattern, they were always extended to full deflection symmetrically — that is with equal deflection of the brakes above and below the fuselage. Aside from a very mild trim change there was no undesirable aircraft motion at all and the speed brakes in the aeroplane were extremely effective; there was never a report of buffet due to speed brake deflection on any flight. The lateral deflection in the aeroplane was effected by the differential deflection of the horizontal stabilizer, the so-called rolling tail. There were no ailerons or spoilers, no device on the wing for aerodynamic roll control. We considered it excellent; there were no undesirable aircraft motions coupled in any axis because of lateral control deflection.

'The stability augmentation system provided rate damping on all three axes. We used moderate gains for all dampers early in the programme and then as we started getting above 3.5M we all expressed an opinion for much higher gains. Of course without the roll damper we could run into serious trouble and uncontrollable areas at high angles of attack, but the rest of the damping system did not matter.

'The side control stick caused a lot of critical analysis because we were departing from a conventional control, but as we got experience using the side stick everything that we felt was controversial became quite satisfactory. All the pilots agreed on its utility at high acceleration and we had one comment about the location of the control; some people, depending on the length of their arms, would complain about just where one arm would fit when they put it down, so we provided a changing position. You could pre-set it before flight to suit the individual pilot. It had five different positions so that made the pilots very happy.

'Throughout the entire programme it was rather nice working with this machine. It was not something we were worrying about putting into production, so as we felt we needed changes in displays, control switches etc we said what we wanted and it was accomplished. So the pilot had a cockpit that was exactly the way he liked it and, surprisingly, the pilots that were flying the aeroplane generally had unanimous agreement when they wanted changes or other indications in the display systems. It was quite delightful. So we considered the side control desirable; then as we progressed in the programme we ended up using the side stick control completely from launch right through to the landing.

'The landing area received a great deal of consideration in the beginning. There was a lot of concern and attention about it until it finally developed into a routine operation based on the experience, procedures and techniques that we began to develop and employ. Before and during the X-15 programme we gave ourselves the benefit of landing simulation by using an F-104 aeroplane. We had predetermined settings of the lift and drag devices and the engine thrust. We could match the lift/drag ratio to that of the X-15 so pilots were therefore able to fly their simulated flame-out patterns, establish the geographic checkpoints and the key altitudes around the pattern and become familiar with the position and timing required in the pattern by the low lift/drag ratio. As a matter of fact, on my first X-15 landing I actually felt as if I had been there before because the 104 provided an excellent tool for us. Of course, there was a wide range of conditions existing in the altitude of the high key point and the lateral dispersions from the touch-down point, but this all indicates a flexibility that the pilot had in manoeuvring to a designated touch-down point.

'We normally flew the aeroplane at 300 kt throughout the flame-out pattern. Ideally, it was nice if you started at about 26,000 to

30,000 ft above the surface. The control system in the aeroplane was absolutely superb and was one of the finest control systems I have had the pleasure to use. If less sink rate was required the aircraft could be flown at an indicated airspeed of 240 kt for best lift/drag, and if necessary excess altitude could be lost at constant airspeed by using the speed brakes. We had sink rates that averaged anywhere from 250 ft per second and some were as high as 474 ft per second, but none of the pilots considered these values to have been a limiting factor in the pattern.

'Aside from the airspeed control all the pilots' cues were external, everything outside the aeroplane except checking the air speed and altitude. We began keeping specific records on the flare altitude; we had data on this and it was varying all over the place. The pilot began to make his flare where he thought it was best; if it was down a little lower it would require a higher g flare, a little bit higher and you had an average g, but it did not seem to make any difference. On a lot of the flights, as we began flying the aeroplane more often, it was significant to see the flare speeds increase as we came round the pattern at 300 kt. Perhaps on the last part of the final approach the speed would increase to 325 kt and they asked very pertinent questions as to why we were doing this.

'It was not to find better handling qualities at high speed, which were completely good throughout this region, but to gain more time after the flare to make the configuration changes, because once you flared you would put the flaps and the gear down. It would allow you more time to make the configuration changes and correct any trim changes and then go ahead and complete the landing at some acceptable values of angle of attack and sink rate and approximately at the intended landing point. The majority of the landings were accomplished with vertical velocities of less than five feet a second and angles of attack between six and eight degrees. Ground effect was not a significant factor. We had a block of twenty landings, measuring our dispersion from an intended touchdown point from a high sink rate dead-stick situation under ideal conditions, as far as weather and airfield were concerned, and we found that all landings occurred within plus or minus twelve hundred feet of that spot. Most of them were considerably closer. In our view, this was quite a good average.'

The X-15, which flew to an altitude of 67 miles and reached a speed of 6.72M (4,520 mph) before its programme ended, laid the foundation for all future hypersonic flight. Its wealth of research documentation, to which was added the experience gained with lifting body projects such as the Northrop M2-F2/F3 and the HL-10, as well as the Martin X-24A/B, was to lead directly to the design of the Space Shuttle. It is fitting that Edwards Air Force Base, from where the X-15 research programme was directed, is now the world's first spaceport; it was here that the Shuttle landed following its first series of routine space missions.

If the Soviet Union and the United States continue to build up their space arsenals, the development of manned combat machines for use in low earth orbit will become a certainty. No one — except perhaps designers working in strict secrecy — can predict what such craft will be like, nor how they would be used operationally. On the other hand, by following present trends we can predict with a great deal of certainty the nature of future combat aircraft designed to operate at less extreme altitudes, and the extent to which traditional pilot tasks will be superseded by automation.

The USAF's projected Advanced Tactical Fighter, which will do in the early part of the 21st century what the F-15 is doing now, is a good example, and as far as its pilots are concerned the keynote will be simplicity. First World War aircraft cockpits contained only ten to fifteen controls and instruments; fighters in the Second World War had about 35. Today's F-15, on the other hand, has more than 300 dials, bells, buzzers, lights and switches; the pilots of this and other modern combat aircraft have reached saturation point, and the trend has got to be away from that.

To test the concepts that will eventually reach fruition in the ATF, the USAF has been following a series of parallel research programmes. The first was the YF-16 control-configured vehicle (CCV) which flew in 1976–77 and demonstrated the decoupled control of aircraft flight path and attitude; in other words the machine could skid sideways, turn without banking, climb or descend without changing its attitude, and point its nose left or right or up or down without changing its flight path.

A second research programme involved HiMAT, a highly manoeuvrable remotely-piloted research aircraft built by Rockwell. HiMAT, which first flew in July 1979, was a scale model of a 1990s ATF design and was required to demonstrate the manoeuvring performance of such an aircraft, which would need to be capable of a sustained 8 g turn at 30,000 ft and 0.9M. The 3,400 lb, 20 ft-long test vehicle was carried into the air on a pylon under the wing of a B-52 and launched at 0.7M at an altitude of between 40,000 and

45,000 ft, landing on Rogers Dry Lake at Edwards AFB at the end of its hour-long sortie.

The whole operation, from launch to landing, was under the control of a ground-based pilot who sat in front of a console containing a full set of flight controls and instruments. Inputs were telemetered from the ground-based computer, which was programmed with the flight characteristics and simulated control system of the aircraft, to the primary on-board processor which drove the digital fly-by-wire control system. Data telemetered from

What might turn out to be the prototype of tomorrow's supersonic V/STOL fighter: a Harrier fitted with a Rolls-Royce Pegasus engine equipped for plenum chamber burning being tested on a special rig at Shoeburyness in 1984.

the aircraft included input for the flight instruments, sampled 55 times a second, accelerations, pitch, roll and yaw rates and angle of attack and sideslip, which were sampled 220 times a second. This high data sampling rate was designed to give the ground controller instantaneous feel of the aircraft's control system, necessary in the handling of precision manoeuvres.

Back-up control on every HiMAT flight was provided by a TF-104 chase aircraft, whose pilot could exercise limited authority through the test vehicle's autopilot. If the control system was switched from normal to back-up, the autopilot took over and HiMAT executed a programmed recovery manoeuvre, returning to level flight. The vehicle then entered a constant-speed, constant-altitude orbit, maintaining a 35° bank. The TF-104 pilot then took over, using discrete signals to control throttle, left or right turn, dive or climb, orbit or exit orbit and normal or landing flight mode. The approach to land was controlled by the ground pilot with the aid of a TV camera mounted in HiMAT's cockpit position, and the touchdown on steel landing skids was made at the relatively high airspeed of 220 kt.

These and other research programmes, together with advances in software development, will give the ATF pilot an aircraft that is straight out of Star Wars. It will be a single-seat aircraft in which the pilot's sole function is to manage his systems, which will virtually operate by themselves. He will sit in a cockpit dominated by graphic colour displays, and will communicate with these by voice or touch. Displays of this kind, which provide computer-generated pictorial formats for vertical, horizontal and tactical situations, are now being evaluated under the USAF's 'Magic' (Microcomputer Applications of Graphics and Interactive Communications) programme. In the futuristic ATF, a mere handful of colour CRT or flat-screen liquid-crystal displays could replace ninety per cent of the dials and controls found on current instrument panels. Pilot and aircraft will 'talk' to one another, too; voice command will be used for functions such as communications, navigation and stores management, while a synthetic voice will warn the pilot of any important instrument fluctuation or problem while he is looking outside the cockpit.

The ATF pilot will also have the benefit of a flight control system that is highly reliable and resistant to a high degree of damage. The engine and weapon systems will be integrated with flight control, which will probably be of the triplex digital type. One major advantage of this flight control system is that it is self-repairing; if a control surface is lost through battle damage or actuator failure the system automatically reconfigures the remaining surfaces to compensate. At present, an aircraft hit by 37 mm anti-aircraft fire has a ten per cent chance of survival, but a self-repairing control system could increase this to ninety per cent.

The self-repairing control system will have what is known as 'positive pilot alerting'; in other words, if the system sustains damage it tells the pilot not only what has happened, but what tasks the aircraft is now capable of performing. It will inform the pilot whether the damage recovery process is sufficiently effective to allow the aircraft to complete its planned mission, whether it is capable of only performing a secondary mission, whether — if neither alternative is possible — it can recover to a friendly airfield, or where the pilot can eject over friendly territory if he has no other option.

The ATF's integrated flight and fire control (IFFC) system has already been tested in an F-15, which has demonstrated head-on gun attacks against high-speed aircraft, with an optical sensor/tracker pod supplying target trajectory data direct to the flight control system. As long ago as August 1982, a test F-15 was shooting down supersonic target drones head-on after engaging IFFC, and the system has advanced some way since then. For the low-level attack role, the ATF will be fitted with an integrated automatic terrain-following/avoidance and threat avoidance system. This will simultaneously perform vertical terrain following and lateral terrain avoidance, as well as threat avoidance options ranging from evasion, through active and passive counter-measures, to lethal suppression. The ATF will also be stealth-configured, which will greatly enhance its survival prospects in a hostile environment.

It has been said that a good pilot must become part of his aircraft. With ATF this comment takes on a new significance, because ATF will be a 'thinking aircraft' in which pilot and automatic systems will be fully symbiotic with one another. Where military aviation will go beyond it is anybody's guess.

Index